The Clark-Van Til Controversy

The Clark-Van Til Controversy

Herman Hoeksema

The Trinity Foundation

Published by
The Trinity Foundation
Post Office Box 68
Unicoi, Tennessee 37692
http://www.trinityfoundation.org/
ISBN: 0-940931-70-2

Contents

Foreword

THESE essays – which here assume the form of a book for the first time – are editorials from *The Standard Bearer*, the denominational magazine of the Protestant Reformed Churches, published in the mid-1940s. The writer, as well as most of those mentioned in the editorials, has departed this life, but the doctrines discussed in the editorials remain very much with us.

In 1944 the Presbytery of Philadelphia of the Orthodox Presbyterian Church ordained Dr. Gordon Haddon Clark to the ministry of that church. Dr. Clark had been ordained a ruling elder in the Presbyterian church in the 1920s – the church of John Witherspoon, Charles Hodge, and Benjamin Warfield – and, despite his youth, had been in the forefront of the battle then raging against liberalism and modernism. His father was a Presbyterian minister, and his father's father before him.

After earning his Ph.D. in ancient philosophy at the University of Pennsylvania in 1929, and while still teaching at the University, Dr. Clark worked with J. Gresham Machen in organizing the Presbyterian Church of America, later known as the Orthodox Presbyterian Church. Dr. Clark, in fact, nominated Machen for moderator of the PCA (OPC) at the convening of its first General Assembly in June 1936.*

---

* The churlishness of some in the Van Til faction may be seen in the absence of any mention of Dr. Clark – his association with Machen in the founding of the

7

Though Dr. Clark's academic, theological, and ecclesiastical credentials were impeccable, he had never attended seminary. By 1944 Dr. Clark's lack of seminary attendance was a stumblingblock to some in the OPC. This lacuna in Dr. Clark's schooling – but not in his education – became an issue in the acrimonious debate that followed, for most of those who sought to depose Dr. Clark from the ministry – through administrative, not judicial, action, please note – were instructors at Westminster Theological Seminary. Dr. Clark's ordination to the ministry represented a threat to their monopoly on the ministry; they were the gatekeepers, and they perceived Dr. Clark as a dangerous interloper.

The effort, first to prevent his ordination (in 1943) and, that failing, to defrock Dr. Clark raised some serious doctrinal issues, as well as some ugly ecclesiastical politics. It is those doctrinal issues that are the principal concern of these editorials. The Clark-Van Til controversy involved four major issues and several minor ones. The four major doctrinal differences between those who opposed Dr. Clark – the Complainants – and Dr. Clark himself concerned (1) the meaning of the "incomprehensibility" of God; (2) the relationship between divine sovereignty and human responsibility; (3) the doctrine of reprobation versus the "sincere offer" of salvation to the reprobate; and (4) the relationship of the intellect to the will and emotions. The controversy, begun by the Westminster Seminary faculty led by Cornelius Van Til, raged for years; it was finally settled in 1948. Dr. Clark was not deposed from the ministry and both the Complainants and the Presbytery of Philadelphia were scolded for their behavior.

PCA (OPC), his combating modernism, his nominating Machen for Moderator of the General Assembly – in Ned Stonehouse's biography of Machen.

The controversy, sadly, did not end there, simply because the Complainants would not let it end. As soon as Dr. Clark had been vindicated, some among the Complainants announced their intention to harass one of Dr. Clark's principal defenders in the controversy, minister and missionary Dr. Floyd Hamilton. At this point, those who for years had endured the slings and arrows of outrageous theologians called it quits. Realizing that the Westminster Seminary faction would never pursue the peace or purity of the church, even after its highest court had spoken, many of those who had defended Dr. Clark left the OPC. The OPC has never recovered from that loss, and indeed, Christianity in America suffered a serious blow. The two institutions that J. Gresham Machen had founded or helped to found – the independent Westminster Theological Seminary and the Orthodox Presbyterian Church – were at war with each other. One-third of the church walked out the door, including one of its largest congregations.

But God has his own purposes for causing such controversies. The Clark-Van Til controversy provoked one of the most brilliant Christian minds of the twentieth century to focus on some fundamental issues of Christian theology. Over the years that followed, and in a series of irrefragable books, Dr. Clark worked out the Scriptural doctrines of the incomprehensibility of God, the relationship of intellect to will, the relationship of truth to action, the logical dependence of human responsibility on divine sovereignty, the Biblical model of evangelism, and many more related issues. The result is a large body of writing in both theology and philosophy that is unmatched for its soundness, truthfulness, and clarity – an intellectual arsenal that will equip all future defenders of the faith, and a scholarly vein of gold that will support generations of Christian scholars.

While Dr. Clark was writing his seminal books, Dr. Van Til continued to misrepresent Dr. Clark's views to his seminary students, despite Dr. Clark's repeated requests to him to desist. Some of Dr. Van Til's students, to this very day, have persisted in foolishly carrying on the campaign against Dr. Clark. The good that men do is oft interred with their bones, but their bad theology and example live long after them.

In order to help set the record straight about the Clark-Van Til controversy, and to oppose some of Van Til's students who are still parroting the errors of their mentor as well as committing their own errors, we offer these editorial comments from an observer who was a brilliant theologian in his own right, who had no connection with either Dr. Clark or the Orthodox Presbyterian Church, and who saw, quite clearly, the theological roots and logical consequences of the views adopted by the Complainants. Should the reader desire further information about this controversy, he may consult my booklet, *Cornelius Van Til: The Man and the Myth*, and the official records of the Orthodox Presbyterian Church.

John W. Robbins
September 2005

The Clark-Van Til Controversy

Herman Hoeksema

1. Introduction: *The Text of a Complaint*

The above is the title of a lengthy printed protest by some members of the Orthodox Presbyterian Church "against actions of the Presbytery of Philadelphia in the Matter of the Licensure and Ordination of Dr. Gordon H. Clark."

I had read about the controversy involved in *The Presbyterian Guardian*, but I had not seen the complete text of this protest. A friend was kind enough to send it to me, for the which I hereby offer him my sincere thanks.

It appears that on July 7, 1944, a special meeting of the Presbytery of Philadelphia was held, for the purpose of examining a certain Dr. Gordon H. Clark with a view to his licensure and ordination to the ministry. Against the fact that this meeting was called, as well as against its proceedings and decisions, the protest or "Complaint" is directed. It is signed by a dozen signatures, among which are the names of some well known to us: R. B. Kuiper, C. Van Til, and N. B. Stonehouse.

The first part of the *Complaint* concerns the calling of the special meeting. The protestants maintain that the meeting was illegally called, and conclude this part of their protest with the "request that the meeting of the Presbytery of Philadelphia held on July 7, 1944, be found to have been illegally convened and that its acts and decisions and the acts and decisions issuing therefrom be declared null and void" (2).

The rest of the protest, its main body, is divided into four parts, according as it discovers four serious errors in the theological conceptions of Dr. Clark – errors that became manifest, according to the complainants, in Dr. Clark's examination by the Presbytery, and in spite of which fact said Presbytery decided to license him and proceed to his ordination.

The first part deals with Dr. Clark's alleged erroneous views concerning the incomprehensibility and knowability of God (2-6).

The second part concerns Dr. Clark's "view of the relation of the faculty of knowledge, the intellectual faculty, to other faculties of the soul" (6-10).

The third part accuses Dr. Clark of maintaining "that the relationship of divine sovereignty and human responsibility to each other presents no difficulty for his thinking and that the two are easily reconcilable before the bar of human reason" (10-13).

The fourth part is an elaboration upon the statement that "in the course of Dr. Clark's examination it became abundantly clear that his rationalism keeps him from doing justice to the precious teaching of Scripture that in the Gospel God sincerely offers salvation in Christ to all who hear, reprobate as well as elect, and that he has no pleasure in any one's rejecting this offer but, contrariwise, would have all who hear accept it and be saved" (13-15).

Especially in view of the last alleged error of Dr. Clark, the reader can readily understand that we are rather interested in this controversy, and that we cannot refrain from making a few remarks about this *Complaint*.

2. The Views of Gordon H. Clark

In briefly discussing the *Complaint* of some brethren in the Orthodox Presbyterian Church against the Presbytery of Philadelphia in the matter of the examination and licensing of Dr. Gordon H. Clark, I wish it to be understood that I have no intention of defending the views of the latter, for the simple reason that I am not sufficiently acquainted with them.

I confess that the *Complaint* has left the impression on me that, perhaps, in this controversy I would rather take the side of the accused than that of the accusers.

Besides, I read some statements, reputedly of Dr. Clark, with which I heartily agree. For instance, in the little pamphlet entitled *Hints for Personal Workers*, which I am informed is written by Dr. Clark, I find the following statements:

> Sin, however, is worse than a disease. It is true that the Scriptures sometimes speak of sin as a sickness, and of salvation as healing and health. But the Scriptures more fully reveal man's condition when they speak of sin as death, and of salvation as eternal life. In dealing with the sinner, therefore, it is necessary to remember that he cannot be left alone to recuperate, but that, dead in sins, he must be raised to newness of life.
>
> Scripture is very explicit in teaching that all men are born in sin, and are incapable of doing any spiritual good. *Proverbs* 21:4 says, *the plowing of the wicked is sin.* Plowing is here taken as an example of ordinary daily occupations, and the verse means that no matter what an unregenerate person does, he is sinning....
>
> Some earnest Christian workers, not well instructed in the Scriptures, unintentionally pollute the Gospel by denying the awful sinfulness of man. They say that the will of man is free, that he can accept Christ and please God, if only he uses enough will-power. They claim, in effect, that while most of man's nature needs to be re-generated, his will is unaffected or only slightly affected by sin, and so does not need the almighty regenerating power of the Holy Ghost.

These Christian workers will tell a sinner that if he first puts faith in Christ and His promises, God will then regenerate him. Thus they make the human will the initial cause of regeneration. Thus they teach that before regeneration, a sinner can have faith in Christ; that man is not dead in sins, but only partly so; and that the part that is not dead, with some cooperation from God to be sure, can save the other part....

Man cannot of himself will to exercise faith in God. Faith in God is a good act, not a sinful act; and the unregenerate cannot perform good acts – even their plowing is sinful. The Scripture uniformly presents faith in Christ as a gift of God: a gift, be it noted, that he does not give to all men....

The Christian worker, then, must pray that God will regenerate the hearts of his hearers; he must depend neither upon his own powers of persuasion nor upon the sinner's will. He must faithfully present Christ crucified *according to the Scriptures*, being assured that the word of God will not return void, but will accomplish that whereto God sent it.

Let us, then, give all the glory to God, and not divide the glory with a sinful human will.

One receives the impression from these statements that the writer cannot be very far from the kingdom of God, and that, in part at least, the criticism of his accusers is due to the fact that the latter viewed him from the standpoint of the Christian Reformed "Three Points," as is evident from *The Text of a Complaint*.

On the other hand, in a pamphlet also attributed to Dr. Clark entitled *His People*, in which the author defends the doctrine that Christ atoned only for the elect, we find the following statements:

There is of course a sense in which Christ died for all men. He is the propitiation for the sins of the whole world, as this same John tells us in his first epistle. No greater sacrifice would be needed even if all men were to be saved. But obviously Christ is not the propitiation for all sin in the sense that he saves all men, but only in a vague, general sense....

And why, may one ask, does any true Christian, even when emphasizing the general propitiation for all sins, wish to conceal the particular grace and election of God by which God chose him specially and personally out of a mass of lost mankind? We who were chosen in Christ before the foundation of the world are his people whom he came to save. To God alone be all the glory.

Now, if I were to formulate a complaint against Dr. Clark, I would surely attack his somewhat dark theory of general propitiation. But the complainants themselves, evidently, did not consider this in conflict with the Reformed view. It may be worth while to examine the views of the complainants as they are expressed in *The Text of a Complaint.*

But this must wait till our next issue.

3. The Incomprehensibility of God

The first point of the *Complaint* concerns the doctrine of the incomprehensibility of God.

The complainants first rather elaborately explain that the doctrine that God, though knowable, is incomprehensible, is taught by all Reformed theologians, maintained by the Confessions and clearly based on Scripture. This part is rather clear, and easy to follow. Nor is one liable to differ with the complainants on this point.

When, however, they proceed to compare Dr. Clark's teaching on this score with what they claim to be their own, and, of course, the orthodox conception of the incomprehensibility of God, it is not so easy to follow them, and to discover just wherein lies the accused's heterodoxy.

The trouble, in part, appears to be that Dr. Clark's view does not involve an outright denial of God's incomprehensibility. Both he and the complainants admit that God cannot be comprehended. The difference between them, therefore, rather concerns the question as to just what must be understood by the incomprehensibility of God. And this renders the whole dispute rather abstract – a matter, it would seem, to be discussed by a conference of theologians rather than to be used as a ground for protest against the the licensure of a candidate for the ministry. Write the complainants:

> It is true indeed that Dr. Clark accepts the term "incomprehensible" as a quality of God. [This is rather carelessly expressed. One cannot very well accept a *term* as a quality, though one might accept that a *term denotes* a real quality. – H.H.] But the issue of course is not settled by the bare acceptance of the language of the standards.... It is our contention that Dr. Clark's view of the incomprehensibility of God is definitely at variance with the meaning that this doctrine has in Christian theology [5].

What, then, is the exact point of difference?

According to the complainants, it is this, that, while they hold that the difference between the contents of the knowledge of God and the contents of our knowledge is both qualitative and quantitative, Dr. Clark insists that it is only quantitative. And here the complainants mention three specific points of difference between Dr. Clark's view and their own:

1. According to Dr. Clark all truth, in God and in man, is propositional, *i.e.*, assumes the form of propositions (God

is good, man is mortal, two times two are four, the whole is greater than any of its parts, etc. – H. H.). The complainants deny this, at least with regard to God's knowledge.

2. Dr. Clark holds that man's knowledge of any proposition is identical with God's knowledge of the same proposition. Any proposition has the same meaning for God as for man. The complainants deny this. As an item of interest we may mention here that during the examination of Dr. Clark by the Presbytery of Philadelphia the question was asked him: "You would say then, that all that is revealed in the Scripture is capable of being comprehended by the mind of man?" And the answer was given by him: "Oh yes, that is what it is given us for, to understand it" (5).

3. Dr. Clark teaches that God's knowledge consists of an *infinite number* of propositions, while only a finite number can ever be revealed to man. And this shows that, according to him, the difference between God's knowledge and man's knowledge is only quantitative: God simply knows infinitely *more* than man. The complainants insist that it is also qualitative: It also concerns the question as to the *nature* and *mode* of God's knowledge and ours.

Yet, it does not seem certain that Dr. Clark himself would subscribe to this presentation of his views by his opponents. They themselves state: "At other points, indeed, Dr. Clark seems to be employing a different conception of infinity, as when he states that the attributes are infinite as being limited by nothing outside of himself." And again: "he freely recognizes a fundamental difference between the *mode* of God's knowledge and that of man's knowledge." To be more clear on this point we will have to wait for the answer that is being prepared to this *Complaint* by the Presbytery of Philadelphia, which we hope to receive.

However, even now one begins to wonder whether the real

question in this controversy is not whether *God*, but whether his *revelation* to us in the Scriptures, is comprehensible, that is, can be logically understood by the mind of man. Dr. Clark's position is that all of Scripture is given us that we might understand it, that all of it is adapted to our human mind, so that, even though there be many things in that revelation of God which we cannot *fathom*, there is nothing in it that is *contrary* to human intelligence and logic. And the opponents appear to deny this.

And if this should be the real, underlying issue, if the complainants take the stand that Scripture reveals things that are, not above and far beyond, but *contrary* to, in conflict with the human mind, it is my conviction that the complainants should be indicted of heterodoxy, and of undermining all sound theology.

Either the *logic* of revelation is *our* logic, or there is no revelation.

This proposition I am prepared to defend at any time.

4. *The Answer*

The committee appointed by the Presbytery of Philadelphia to prepare an answer to *The Text of a Complaint*, has finished its task, and through the kindness of one of the committee members, I received, upon request, a copy of the proposed *Answer*. My hearty thanks for this kindness.

The Answer is a pamphlet consisting of almost forty pages. Its form is neat. Its contents are lucid. One does not have to guess just what the committee means. As to its order, it naturally follows the various points advanced in the *Complaint*. The first point, that concerning the incomprehensibility of God, receives the lion's share of the attention of the committee.

Since I received this copy of *The Answer* while I was discussing the first point of the *Complaint,* the former arrived just in time for me to combine the two in my discussion. By following this method we will more readily obtain a clear conception of the difference between the position of the complainants and that of the respondents.

Let us learn, then, from *The Answer* just what is Dr. Clark's view of the incomprehensibility of God. We quote:

> The view of the *Complaint* is that "*God because of his very nature* must remain incomprehensible to man"; it is "not the doctrine that God can be known only if he makes himself known and in so far as he makes himself known." Moreover, all knowledge which man can attain differs from the knowledge of God "in a qualitative sense and not merely in degree." Thus God's knowledge and man's knowledge do not "coincide at a single point." A proposition does not "have the same meaning for man as for God." Man's knowledge is "analogical to the knowledge God possesses, but it can never be identified with the knowledge" which God "possesses of the same proposition." "The divine knowledge as *divine* transcends human knowledge as human, even when that human knowledge is a knowledge communicated by God." "*Because of his very nature as infinite and absolute* the knowledge which God possesses of himself and of all things must remain a mystery which the finite mind cannot penetrate." This latter statement does not mean merely that man cannot penetrate this mystery unaided by revelation: It means that even revelation by God could not make man understand the mystery, for the preceding sentences assert that it is the nature of God that renders him incomprehensible, not the lack of a revelation about it. As the analysis proceeds, these quotations with the argument from which they are taken will be seen to imply two chief points. First, there is some truth that

God cannot put into propositional form; this portion of truth cannot be expressed conceptually. Second, the portion of truth that God can express in propositional form never has the same meaning for man as it has for God. Every proposition that man knows has a qualitatively different meaning for God. Man can grasp only an analogy of the truth, which, because it is an analogy, is not the truth itself.

On the other hand, Dr. Clark contends that the doctrine of the incomprehensibility of God as set forth in Scripture and in the *Confession of Faith* includes the following points: 1. The essence of God's being is incomprehensible to man except as God reveals truths concerning his own nature. 2. The manner of God's knowing, an eternal intuition, is impossible for man. 3. Man can never know exhaustively and completely God's knowledge of any truth in all its relationships and implications; because every truth has an infinite number of relationships and implications, and since each of these implications in turn has other infinite implications, these must ever, even in Heaven, remain inexhaustible for man. 4. But, Dr. Clark maintains, the doctrine of the incomprehensibility of God does not mean that a proposition, *e.g.*, two times two are four, has one meaning for man and a tentatively different meaning for God, or that some truth is conceptual and other truth is non-conceptual in nature [9, 19].

This, according to the committee, is "the crux of the issue." They have a good deal more to say in defense of Dr. Clark's position, but we need not quote more. We rather make a few remarks:

1. It still seems to me that the question involved, considered by itself, would be a very interesting subject for a theological conference, rather than a basis for complaint against the licensure of a candidate for the ministry. Of course, if this

first point of the *Complaint* is introduced here as a basis for what follows, and if it was the real purpose of the complainants to persuade the Orthodox Presbyterian Church to adopt the Arminian doctrine of the Christian Reformed Church as expressed by the Synod of Kalamazoo in 1924, particularly the view that God is gracious to the reprobate, and that the preaching of the Gospel is a well-meaning offer of salvation on the part of God to all men – in other words, the doctrine that God sincerely seeks the salvation of those whom He will not save – this first point is quite important. For this Christian Reformed doctrine, itself a plain contradiction, is based on the contention that there are contradictions in Scripture, and that it is possible for faith to accept contradictions, that is, you understand, contradictions for man's mind, not for God. And in that light one can understand that the complainants must maintain the position: *A proposition does not have the same meaning for God as for man.* The *Complaint* leaves the impression that it was chiefly written by Christian Reformed men that are trying to defend the Christian Reformed tradition in the Orthodox Presbyterian Church and to introduce into the latter the errors of 1924. In fact, this impression is so strong that I make bold to conjecture that the *Complaint* was written by more than one author, and that I could point out the writer of the last part merely on the basis of internal evidence. I would consider it deplorable if the Orthodox Presbyterian Church would yield to this temptation.

2. From *The Answer* it is plain that the issue does not concern the truth of God's incomprehensibility as such, but an interpretation of that doctrine. And I agree with *The Answer* when it states that the complainants make a false claim when they insist "that throughout Christian theology this doctrine has but one definite meaning," that theirs, the complainants', view "is that one definite meaning, and that Dr. Clark in dis-

agreeing with them rejects this uniform element in Christian theology" (8, 9).

3. To say that any proposition does not have the same meaning for God as it has for man is, it appears to me: (1) A rationalistic contention. The complainants do not derive this proposition from Scripture, nor will they ever be able to find Scriptural ground for it. (2) A statement which can only mean that we can never know the truth about anything. Certain it is that the meaning a proposition has for God is the only true meaning; if for us it has another meaning, we simply have not the truth. (3) A denial of the truth of revelation. That our knowledge of God is finite, and that even through revelation we can never comprehend God, the infinite One, has always been held by all theologians. But if what God revealed to us has a different meaning for Him than for us, God is not only incomprehensible, but also unknowable. Then revelation itself is not true and reliable.

4. And so, it still seems to me that the issue between the complainants and the Presbytery of Philadelphia is not the incomprehensibility of God, but the question whether revelation itself is intelligible to us. To deny the latter is to destroy the very foundations of theology.

5. The Primacy of the Truth

The second main point of the *Complaint* against Dr. Clark concerns, in the words of the complainants, "his view of the relation of the faculty of knowledge, the intellectual faculty, to other faculties of the soul." I have re-read the material the complainants offer on this point, and also its refutation in *The Answer*. I think that the points of difference between Dr. Clark and his accusers may, in the main, be summarized as follows:

1. The complainants hold to the trichotomous division or distinction of the human soul into its faculties, and apply this also to God. In the human soul they distinguish between *intellect, emotion*, and *will*. Dr. Clark prefers the dichotomous distinction of *intellect* and *will*, refuses to speak of emotion as a separate faculty, and considers the emotions as aspects of the intellect and will. And he, too, applies this distinction to God. This seems evident from the *Complaint*:

> Any statement of the relation between the intellectual and the other spiritual faculties must needs be concerned with God as well as with man. Although comparatively little was said in the course of Dr. Clark's examination about what might be called divine psychology, there is enough evidence in the transcript of the examination to outline his position. Dr. Clark should certainly not be accused of dividing the nature of God, or even of man, into discrete parts which might be labeled "intellect," "emotion," and "volition," or by other terms. However, since he is willing, at least for the sake of argument, to use such words as indicating different faculties, there is certainly meaning in what has been said on the subject. First of all, Dr. Clark specifically states [16] that the statement of the *Westminster Confession* that "God is without...passions" means that God is lacking in feeling and emotion. Although he objects to a definition of *feeling* or *emotion* which would make those words mean anything different from "passions," he does not make provision for any other faculty in God's nature which would be non-intellectual and non-volitional. Secondly, to round out the picture, Dr. Clark apparently does assume that God has both intellectual and volitional faculties, for he talks about the decretive and preceptive will of God, as well as about God's knowledge [7].

The Answer makes plain that Dr. Clark does not deny the reality of emotions in God, but gives them a different connotation from that of the complainants, and assigns to them a position different from that which the latter assign to them, in relation to God's intellect and will. The complainants make of the emotions in God a separate faculty, next to, and on a level with intellect and will. Dr. Clark gives them a subordinate position, and explains them as aspects or functions of God's intellect and will. From *The Answer* we quote:

> Dr. Clark never made any "forthright denial of any-
> thing that might be called emotion in God." Love or
> wrath "might be called an emotion." Dr. Clark did not
> deny love and wrath to God. He holds that while some
> people might call God's love and wrath emotions, it is
> better to classify them as volitions. In this Dr. Clark is in
> accord with a large section of theology and of literary
> usage [27].

It would seem, then, that the chief point of difference between the complainants and Dr. Clark may be stated thus, that the former hold to the trichotomous, the latter to the dichotomous, distinction as applied to human and "divine psychology." (I must not be held responsible for the latter term.)

2. While the complainants place the intellect, emotions, and will, both in man and in God, on a level (they even leave the impression of teaching a certain primacy of the emotions), Dr. Clark certainly assigns to the emotions a subordinate position, and according to the complainants, teaches the primacy of the intellect. The latter position the complainants hold to be a serious error, contrary to the best Reformed tradition. I quote from the *Complaint*:

> While Dr. Clark is "willing to admit that the intellect
> and volition and emotion are equally essential to a human

26

being," he maintains that they have "different functions," and "that the intellect is the supreme function" [7].

What, in the first place, is the Reformed teaching about the aspects of God's nature, or, if you will, the faculties which reside in God? [How easy it would be to deduce from statements like "faculties in God" that the complainants deny the simplicity of God! We do not make the deduction, of course, although we would neither be responsible for the terms. – H.H.] That God has knowledge and will is agreed by all. The questions that must concern us are two: Does God have what may be properly called "emotions"? and, What is the relation between God's faculties? If we assign to the word "emotion" an *a priori* definition which in the nature of the case identifies emotion with "passions," it would obviously be denying our standards to say that God has emotions (*Westminster Confession*, II, 1). God does not change; there is no shadow of turning in him; he is not a man that he should repent; he is immutable. Certainly, also, God does not share certain of the qualities which we call "emotions," such as fear, longing, and surprise. If we are to speak of feeling or emotions in God at all, we must confine ourselves to his attributes, which are sometimes summed up under the word "benevolence": love, goodness, mercy, and grace. Even here we must be careful to defend the immutable self-determination of God. But the question still remains, can these be identified with, or associated with, the idea of "emotion" or "feeling"? Obviously, we define those words in their narrow but perfectly colloquial sense as something which arouses the will and thus determines action. In fine, is there any quality or faculty in God which is neither intellectual nor volitional, and which underlies or accompanies volitional activity? That question, in similar words, Dr. Clark studiously avoided answering [7, 8].

It is interesting for more than one reason to notice how Dr. Clark "studiously avoided answering" this particular question in his examination. In *The Answer* the transcript of the examination of this point is quoted as follows:

Q. When the *Confession of Faith* says: "God is without body, parts, or passions," does it mean that God is lacking in feeling or emotion?

A. It does.

Q. I'll define the meaning of *emotions*: I mean – affections in the sense of principal activity with reference to objections. Now I'll repeat the question, if you wish.

A. Go ahead.

Q. The *Confession* says: "God is without body, parts, or passions." Does it mean that God is lacking in feeling or emotion?

A. Go ahead.

Q. And by *feeling* or *emotion* I mean – in the sense of principal activity with reference to objects.

A. I forget which way to answer that – yes or no.

Q. The *Confession of Faith* says: "God is without body or parts."

A. The answer is yes, but I protest against the awful English in your statement, the word *emotion* – never mind that English.

Q. You mean that God has never acted upon anything aside from himself?

A. I don't understand you.

Q. What I would like to know is this: We can call these feelings or emotions in God, and I would define them as analogous to our feelings and emotions and affections in the sense that they are active principles, active with reference to objects. For example: God is angry with the wicked. God loves His people eternally, would you deny that?

A. That is right, right; what you say is right.

Q. That is what the *Confession* means?

A. No, what – not what it means right there – not what the *Confession* means.

If the transcript of this part of the examination is correct, the insinuation that Dr. Clark "studiously avoided answering" is not true. However, one wonders whether the questioner himself was not somewhat vague and confused in his own mind. And certain it is that the last question was answered correctly by Dr. Clark: When the *Westminster Confession* states that there are no passions in God, it certainly has no reference to God's wrath against the wicked, and to his love to his elect.

Because of lack of space, and because of fear that more of this material might make our readers too dizzy at present, I must reserve my own opinion of this point of the controversy for the next issue.

6. The Primacy of the Intellect

What shall we say about the second part of the *Complaint*, that which is concerned with the faculties of the soul?

First of all, I wish to repeat that also this question might be a nice subject for discussion by some philosophical or theological club. How the Presbytery of Philadelphia could subject a theological candidate to several hours of grilling on this point is, I confess, beyond my comprehension. And still more difficult it is for me to understand how the complainants could discover in Dr. Clark's views in this respect sufficient ground for a protest against his licensure and ordination. The question involved is, to say the least, debatable.

But more must be said.

For one can only be amazed at the claim made by the complainants that their view on this question – the view, namely, that holds the trichotomous distinction between the powers of the soul, and that assigns to the emotions a leading place among the faculties of the soul rather than to the intellect – is historically and currently Reformed or Calvinistic.

I claim that the very opposite is true.

The quotations the complainants offer in their protest to prove their contention are very unconvincing. In fact, they frankly admit

> From the viewpoint of abstract psychology, it is perfectly true that Reformed theologians have not been in complete agreement as to the number and names of the faculties of the human soul. In speaking specifically of the faculties of the human soul, Calvin mentions by name only the intellect and will (*Institutes*, Bk. 1, Chap. XV, Sect. 6). Augustine refers to the perception, understanding, and will [*The Text of a Complaint*, 8].

And again, they admit: "Calvin, who so clearly gives intellect a control over will, though not by virtue of that a primacy over will," etc. (9). But they insist that "the more recent theologians, however, seem to agree in large measure on the threefold distinction of intellect, emotion, and will" (8).

We may note here that the complainants express themselves very carefully: "the more recent theologians *seem* to agree *in large measure*." But even so the complainants are in error. It is far nearer to the truth to state that Reformed theologians have, generally speaking, been strongly opposed to the threefold distinction of intellect, will, and emotion, and have often expressed their fear of the danger of this distinction. The danger of this distinction, to which they usually pointed, is that the emotions in that case gradually assume a dominating and controlling position in the soul of man, and that, according to this trichotomous psychology, such experiences as love and

THE PRIMACY OF THE INTELLECT

hatred, sorrow and joy, repentance and remorse, in fact, all religion and morality are relegated to the emotions or feeling. And that would exactly be the deathblow to all true religion. Reformed theologians were, therefore, usually in favor of the dichotomous distinction of intellect and will, and ascribed the emotions partly to the intellect, and partly to the will. And again, it may be stated without fear of possible contradiction that Reformed theology usually favored the "primacy of the intellect."

I thought, and still think, that this was so well known that I could only be amazed when I discovered that some theologians of Philadelphia took the opposite stand.

Let me offer a quotation or two.

The first is from Bavinck, *Gereformeerde Dogmatiek*, II, 596-597:

> Secondly, to this image of God belong the powers [*vermogens*] of man. While the spirit is the principle, and the soul the subject of life in man, the heart is, according to Scripture, the organ for his life. It is, first, center of his physical life, but next also, metaphorically, the ground and source of all psychical life, of emotions and passions, of desire and will, even of thinking and knowing. Out of the heart are all the THOTSEOTH CHAJIM, issues of life (*Proverbs* 4:23). This life, that has its source in the heart, divides itself into *two currents*. [I underscore. – H.H.] On the one hand, one may distinguish that life which comprises all impressions, notions, sensations, perceptions, considerations, thoughts, knowledge, wisdom, that finds, especially in its higher form, its organ in the *nous* (mind), and embodies itself in the word, in speech. And on the other hand, in the heart have their origin the affections, emotions, passions, inclinations, impulses, desires and determinations of the will, which must be guided by the *nous* (mind) and express themselves in the

act.... Augustine even recognized in the heart, intellect, and will (*memoria, intellectus, voluntas*) an analogy of the trinitarian life of God. Even as the Father gives life to the Son and to the Spirit, and the Spirit proceeds from the Father through the Son, thus also with man it is the heart, the deep, mysterious life of the soul, that gives existence to intellect and will, and that more specifically causes the will to follow the intellect.... but the theology of the West avoided all these errors [of Rationalism, Pelagianism, Mysticism – H.H.]; it is understood that the doctrine of God and of man are closely related; in the trinity it, therefore, maintained the oneness in being, the distinction of the three persons, and the filioque [the procession of the Spirit also from the Son – H.H.], and accordingly, with respect to psychology it taught that the deep and hidden life of the soul becomes manifest only through the intellectual and volitional faculty, and that, as to these two, the latter is led and governed by the former.

This is clear language. Its meaning is not at all ambiguous. Bavinck teaches that there are only two faculties of the soul – intellect and will; and he maintains the primacy of the intellect. What is more, he here states that Western theology, since the days of Augustine, held the same views.

I have no time to look up the exact pages in the *Psychologische Beginselen* by the same author, but if the complainants will take the trouble, they will find a rather interesting discussion of this subject in that work, and a strong condemnation of the trichotomous distinction. Years ago, I delivered a paper on this same subject before a ministers' conference, and I recollect Bavinck's discussion just now referred to distinctly.

The complainants refer, in proof of their contention, to Dr. Kuyper's *Dictaten Dogmatiek*, Volume II, *Locus de Homine*, pages 68-88. But they are mistaken. Dr. Kuyper would be the last one to assign to the emotions the position of a separate faculty. It is true that he speaks of three faculties, but they are the perceptive, the intellectual, and the volitional faculty. Virtually, this means the same as the dichotomous distinction between intellect and will, for the perceptive faculty belongs to the intellect in the broader sense.

That Kuyper was strongly in favor of the "primacy of the intellect" is well known. Even in the very passage to which the complainants refer, he writes:

> Does the will stand under the command of the intellect, or does it operate out of itself?
>
> There has been a controversy about this problem as long as men thought about the responsibility of man. The Mystics say: The will operates out of itself. The pure theologians [*zuivere theologen*] teach: The will stands under the command of the intellect.

On this point of the *Complaint* I must, therefore, maintain: 1. That the complainants have no cause for protest against the licensure of Dr. Clark; and 2. That their own position is in conflict with the general stand of Reformed theologians.

Personally, I believe that there is room for debate, and for further development of the solution of this problem.

7. Rationalism

The third indictment the complainants bring against Dr. Clark is really twofold: According to them, he is a rationalist and an antinomian.

The accusation of rationalism is based on the contention that Dr. Clark tries to solve problems, paradoxes, and contradictions, particularly the problem of the relation between divine sovereignty and human responsibility. Anyone who makes an attempt to solve this problem, who tries to harmonize these two, who claims that this solution is possible – and especially he who is ready to offer his solution of this problem – is, according to the complainants, a rationalist.

We quote from the *Complaint:*

> Dr. Clark asserts that the relationship of divine sovereignty and human responsibility to each other presents no difficulty for his thinking and that the two are easily reconcilable before the bar of human reason. He expresses surprise that so many theologians find an insuperable difficulty here [10].

The complainants then make several quotations from Reformed writers to show that by the theologians of good standing the problem has always been considered insoluble. It presents an apparent contradiction which we are not able to harmonize. Both must be confessed – that God is absolutely sovereign and that man is responsible. But how they are to be harmonized is beyond the understanding of the human mind. Thus they quote from Berkhof, Calvin, Vos, A. A. Hodge, and Abraham Kuyper. And then the complainants continue:

> Here then is a situation which is inadequately described as amazing. There is a problem which has baffled the greatest theologians in history. Not even Holy Scripture offers a solution. But Dr. Clark asserts unblushingly that for his thinking the problem has ceased to be a problem. Here is something phenomenal. What accounts for it? The most charitable, and no doubt the correct, explanation is that Dr. Clark has come under the spell of rationalism. It is difficult indeed to escape the conclusion that by his refusal to permit the scriptural teaching of divine sovereignty and the scriptural teaching of human

responsibility to stand alongside each other and by his claim that he has fully reconciled them with each other before the bar of human reason Dr. Clark has fallen into the error of rationalism. To be sure, he is not a rationalist in the sense that he substitutes human reasoning for divine revelation as such. But, to say nothing of his finding the solution of the problem of the relation to each other of divine sovereignty and human responsibility in the teaching of pagan philosophers who were totally ignorant of the teaching of Holy Writ on either of these subjects, it is clear that Dr. Clark regards Scripture from the viewpoint of a system which to the mind of man must be harmonious in all its parts. The inevitable outcome is rationalism in the interpretation of Scripture. And that too is rationalism. Although Dr. Clark does not claim actually to possess at the present moment the solution of every scriptural paradox, yet his rationalism leaves room at best for only a temporary subjection of human reason to the divine Word... [12].

What shall we say about this accusation of rationalism?

First of all, we may note that it is an old one. There is nothing original in the findings of the complainants. They speak the language of the Christian Reformed leaders since about 1922-1924. From these they have, no doubt, learned to speak their theological language. Personally, we are very familiar with the accusation they now bring against Dr. Clark.

But what of the accusation itself?

The complainants speak of a "situation which is inadequately described as amazing," and of "something phenomenal." I must confess that these words express exactly my sentiment when I read this part of the *Complaint*. There is here, indeed, something that is more than amazing, that is really unbelievable, that might almost be catalogued as another paradox: the phenomenon that theologians accuse a brother theologian of heresy because he tries to solve problems!

For, mark you well, it is exactly this that these complainants do in this part of the *Complaint*. They simply accuse him of trying to find a solution, of claiming to have found a solution. Whether Dr. Clark has actually succeeded or not to discover a solution of the problem of God's sovereignty in relation to man's responsibility is not the question at all. Whether his solution is right or wrong has nothing to do with this part of the *Complaint*. The mere fact that Dr. Clark attempts to harmonize things makes him a heretic, a rationalist. Other theologians have always claimed that the problem is not capable of solution; the complainants themselves insist that in the problem of God's sovereignty and man's responsibility we face a paradox, a contradiction as far as we can see: This should have been sufficient to warn Dr. Clark against the attempt to seek a solution. That he, nevertheless, did make the attempt shows that he is a heretic, a rationalist.

That, as it appears to me, is the whole argument of the complainants.

And this is something which, to my mind, the word *amazing* is inadequate to describe.

But what about the accusation of rationalism?

Is it really rationalism to make the attempt to bring Scripture into harmony with itself?

The complainants maintain that it is:

> Dr. Clark regards Scripture from the viewpoint of a system which to the mind of man must be harmonious in all its parts. The inevitable outcome is rationalism in the interpretation of Scripture. And that too is rationalism.

The language of the complainants is somewhat ambiguous here, whether the ambiguity is intentional or accidental. The words might convey the impression that Dr. Clark begins with a system of thought, not derived from the Scriptures, and that now he proceeds to explain Scripture in such a way as to support that preconceived philosophical system. And that would, indeed, be rationalism. Scripture would then be distorted to fit Dr. Clark's system. But the complainants do not openly accuse him of this. The words may also mean that, according to Dr. Clark's view, there is in the revelation of the Word of God itself a harmonious system of truth, which, by careful exegesis, comparing Scripture with Scripture, the theologian attempts to bring to light and to formulate. And this seems to be the truth. Thus, at least, *The Answer* interprets Dr. Clark's attempt to harmonize divine sovereignty and human responsibility. We quote: "It is pertinent to note that Dr. Clark, instead of approaching these problems on a rationalistic basis, reaches his conclusion from an exegesis of Scripture" (37). And again:

> Next, the attempt to find by a deeper study of the Scripture the solution of paradoxes – a use of exegesis that the complainants call rationalism – is in the eyes of the complainants incompatible with subjection of human reason to the divine Word.... In other words, a man who tries to understand what God has revealed to him cannot be subject to the revelation, and the more he understands, the less he is subject; probably the less he understands, the more subject he is; so that the really obedient and devout man must be completely ignorant. By what right do the complainants imply that the attempt to understand Scripture is inconsistent with believing Scripture? [37].

We may take it, then, that the attempt to harmonize Scripture with itself is, by the complainants, branded as rationalism.

This we absolutely deny.

Let the complainants prove their contention. They do not do this. They do not even make an attempt to prove this charge of rationalism.

The Answer reduces the contention of the complainants, somewhat ironically, to absurdity, by showing that ultimately it leads to the conclusion that "the really obedient and devout man must be completely ignorant."

But if the contention of the complainants is true, it certainly follows that all theology, and especially all dogmatics, is rationalistic, for it proceeds from the assumption that the truth revealed in the Bible can be formulated into a logical system.

No theologian has ever proceeded from the assumption of the complainants. Dogmatics is a system of truth elicited from Scripture. And exegesis always applied the rule of the *regula Scripturae*, which means that throughout the Bible there runs a consistent line of thought in the light of which the darker and more difficult passages must be interpreted. The complainants virtually deny this, at least, and that, too, rather arbitrarily, with relation to the problem of God's sovereignty and man's responsibility.

Who does not know that Reformed theologians have always interpreted those passages of Scripture, which at first sight seem to be in favor of the Arminian view, in the light of the current teaching of Holy Writ that salvation is of the Lord, that grace is sovereign, that the atonement is particular, and that man is not free to do good? According to the contention of the complainants, this is rationalism.

The complainants simply ride a recent Christian Reformed hobby.

As to "contradictions," I maintain that there are no such things in the revelation of God in Scripture, for the simple reason that Scripture teaches us everywhere that God is One, and that he cannot deny himself. His revelation, too, is one, and does not contradict itself.

No, but the complainants would say, there are no *real* contradictions, but there are *apparent* contradictions in the Bible nevertheless, and them we must leave severely alone, without even making an attempt at solution. We must simply and humbly accept them.

I most positively deny all of this.

By *apparent* contradictions the complainants mean propositions or truth that to the human mind, and according to human logic, are contradictory. I deny that there are such propositions in the Bible. If there were, they could not be the object of our faith. It is nonsense to say that we must humbly believe what is contradictory. This is simply impossible. The complainants themselves cannot believe contradictions. Contradictions are propositions that mutually exclude each other, so that the one denies the truth of the other. The principles of contradictions are: 1. That a thing cannot at the same time *be* and *not be*. 2. That a thing must either be or not be. 3. That the same property cannot be affirmed and denied at the same time of the same subject. A is A. A is not Not-A. Everything is either A or Not-A.

I challenge anyone to point out that there are propositions in the Bible that violate these fundamental principles of logic.

I challenge anyone to prove that it is possible for the believer to accept such contradictions, or that it is Christian humility to claim such faith.

Perhaps it may be worth the effort to apply these statements to the problem of God's sovereignty and man's responsibility.

But this must wait until our next issue.

8. Sovereignty and Responsibility

The question is whether there is a real or apparent contradiction involved in the truth of God's sovereignty and man's
responsibility.

Let us put both truths in propositional form:

1. God is absolutely sovereign, even so that he determines
the moral acts of man, both good and evil.

2. Man is responsible before God for all his moral acts.

Now, the question is not whether there is a problem here.
It may well be that we cannot answer the question how God
is able to determine man's deeds without destroying man's
responsibility. That he is able to do so is asserted plainly by
the two propositions stated above. But whether or not we can
understand this operation of the sovereign God upon man is
not the question. The sole question is whether the two propositions concerning God's sovereignty and man's responsibility
are contradictory. This we deny. In fact, they cannot possibly
be, for the simple reason that they assert something about two
wholly different subjects.

They would be contradictory if the first proposition denied
what is affirmed in the second. But this is not true. The first
proposition asserts something about God: He is absolutely
sovereign and determines the acts of man. The second proposition predicates something about man: He is responsible
for his moral acts. Does the first proposition deny that man
is responsible? If it does you have here a contradiction. But
it does not. Those who like to discover a contradiction here,
usually the enemies of the truth of God's sovereignty, simply
take for granted that to assert that God is sovereign even over
man's acts is to say the same as that man is not responsible. It
must be pointed out, however, that this is neither expressed
nor implied in the first proposition. In the two propositions

responsibility is not both affirmed and denied at the same time to man.

The two propositions would, of course, also be contradictory if the second proposition denied what is affirmed in the first. In that case, sovereignty even over the acts of man would be both affirmed and denied to God. But also this is neither expressed nor implied in the two propositions, unless it can first be shown conclusively that to say that man is responsible is the same as declaring that God is not sovereign over his moral acts. And this has never been demonstrated, nor is it self-evident.

If they were really contradictory they could not both be the object of the Christian's faith. We could only conclude that either the one or the other were not true.

Now, however, since they involve no contradiction, and since both are clearly revealed in Scripture, we accept both, whether or not we can combine them into one concept.

And the attempt to do so, to solve the problem, must be considered laudable.

What pastor has not confronted the necessity, in his catechism classes, to answer a question concerning this problem when he was instructing his pupils in the truth of God's immutable decrees? And what instructor was satisfied to reply to his earnest inquiring pupil that here we face a contradiction?

To me it would seem that the solution of the problem, as far as Reformed theology is concerned, must be sought in the direction of properly defining man's responsibility. If the question is asked how a divinely determined creature can be responsible for his acts, it stands to reason that his freedom and responsibility must be defined as falling within the compass of God's decrees and sovereignty. Man's freedom is a creaturely, and, therefore, a dependent freedom. And so is his responsibility.

However this may be, and whether or not Dr. Clark's solution is acceptable, his attempt to solve the problem is laudable. And it is a very strange procedure to accuse a man of heresy because of the very fact that he attempts a solution of a difficult problem.

While the attempt on the part of Dr. Clark to solve this problem is labeled as *rationalism*, the solution he offers is characterized as *antinomianism*. We quote from the *Complaint*:

> The history of doctrine tells us that the view under discussion is far from innocent. The tenet that divine sovereignty and human responsibility are logically reconcilable has been held by two schools of thought, both of which claimed to be Reformed but neither of which was recognized as Reformed by Reformed churches. One of these schools is Arminianism. It meant to uphold both divine sovereignty and human responsibility, especially the latter, but in its rationalistic attempt to harmonize the two it did great violence to the former. The other school is Antinomianism. It also meant to uphold both divine sovereignty and human responsibility, especially the former, but in its rationalistic attempt to harmonize the two it did great violence to the latter. Dr. Abraham Kuyper has described Antinomianism as a "dreadful sin which occurs almost exclusively in the Reformed churches." He says that what accounts for this phenomenon is a one-sided emphasis in much Reformed preaching on God's decretive will at the expense of His preceptive will. He deems it essential to hold that Scripture distinguishes between the sphere of divine sovereignty and the sphere of human responsibility, and "that this distinction is so absolute that one can never pass from the one into the other" (*Dictaten Dogmatiek, Locus de Deo*, part 3, pp. 113*ff*.). In the light of history we cannot but hold that his rationalism exposes Dr. Clark to the peril of Antinomianism.

Here attention must be called to his treatment of human responsibility in the article "Determinism and Responsibility." Reformed theologians generally are exceedingly circumspect when they discuss the relation of the divine decree and divine providence to the sin of man. There is excellent reason for their carefulness. They are zealous to maintain God's holiness as well as His sovereignty, not to detract, after the manner of the Antinomians, from human responsibility. But Dr. Clark says boldly: "Does the view here proposed make God the Author of sin? Why the learned divines who formulated the various creeds so uniformly permitted such a metaphorical expression to becloud the issue is a puzzle. This view certainly makes God the First and Ultimate Cause of everything. But very slight reflection on the definition of responsibility and its implication of a superior authority shows that God is not responsible for sin" (22). It is meaningful that Dr. Clark is not careful to say, as so many Reformed theologians are, that God is not the efficient cause of sin (*e.g.*, Berkhof, *Systematic Theology*, p. 108) [12].

And at the end of this part of the *Complaint* the complainants conclude that Dr. Clark's

> rationalism has resulted in his departing from the historic Reformed doctrine of human responsibility. In his attempt to reconcile by human reason divine sovereignty and human responsibility he has done decided violence to the latter [13].

Dr. Clark, therefore, is an antinomian rationalist, according to the complainants. His refusal to accept contradictions makes him "one-sided."

There is nothing original in this accusation.

It has become rather customary in recent years – especially since the Christian Reformed Synod of 1924 – to explain all

43

forms of heresies as rationalistic attempts to solve contradictions resulting in one-sidedness. This makes it so very easy to classify one whom we seek to expose as a heretic! You can pick out almost any classification you like. Thus, *e.g.*, the undersigned has been labeled an Anabaptist, an Antinomian, an Arminian, a Barthian, etc.

The complainants adopt the same policy.

Arminianism, say they, is the result of a rationalistic attempt to reconcile God's sovereignty and human responsibility. So is Antinomianism. Both become one-sided in their attempt. So Dr. Clark tries to solve the same problem with the same result of one-sidedness on the Antinomian side. Hence, he is an Antinomian.

But is all this true? Or is it merely an attempt – a purely rationalistic attempt too – on the part of the complainants to find a heretical name for Dr. Clark? Is Arminianism really the result of an attempt to "uphold both divine sovereignty and human responsibility" as the complainants claim? Was it not from the very outset an attempt to deny and disprove the doctrine of absolute predestination and of the sovereignty of God in relation to the freedom of man? And is Antinomianism to be explained as an attempt to solve the problem of God's sovereignty and human responsibility? Anyone that is at all acquainted with the facts knows better. It was concerned with the relation of justification and good works and rejected the moral law as binding upon Christians. It is true that many of them were also strong in their emphasis on predestination, but this emphasis also was especially applied to their view of the justification of the elect. But Antinomianism cannot be called a rationalistic attempt to harmonize divine sovereignty and human responsibility. And whatever must be thought of Dr. Clark's attempt to solve this problem, it cannot be branded as Antinomian.

Besides, the indictment that Dr. Clark does violence to or denies the responsibility of man because of his one-sided emphasis on the sovereignty of God is only a conclusion which the complainants draw from some of his statements. Dr. Clark himself would never admit the truth of the conclusion. He never denies the responsibility of man, nor does he ever present God as the real author of human acts, though he insists that he determines them. He maintains only that "determinism is consistent with responsibility," a statement which itself proves that he does not eliminate the responsibility of man in his attempt to harmonize it with God's sovereignty. It is always dangerous to draw conclusions from someone's statements in order then to attribute the conclusions to the author of the statements. Let us not forget that enemies of the truth drew conclusions from Paul's doctrine, accused him of Antinomianism (*Romans* 3:8; 6:1), and of making God the author of sin and denying the responsibility of man (*Romans* 9:19).

It seems to me that this part of the *Complaint* utterly fails to prove its point.

9. The Sincere Offer of the Gospel

The last point of the *Complaint* concerns the so-called sincere offer of salvation on the part of God to all men, particularly to the reprobate.

Here the *Complaint* descends from the stratosphere of philosophical contemplation and theological debate to the lower spheres of plain, even superficial reasoning, where even common mortals that may have been present at the examination of Dr. Clark, and at the subsequent debate about the questions involved, must have felt that they were able to participate in the discussion.

Here, too, the *Complaint* reveals, more clearly than anywhere else, its distinctly Christian Reformed tendency, particularly its sympathy with the three well-known decrees of the Synod of Kalamazoo, 1924.

Because it is especially on this point that the controversy of the Presbytery of Philadelphia, which, as it now appears, is to be continued in the General Assembly of the Orthodox Presbyterian Church, is identical with our own controversy with the Christian Reformed Church in 1924, it may not be superfluous to refresh our memory in this respect, so we will try to analyze the argument of the *Complaint* somewhat in detail.

If the standpoint of Dr. Clark with respect to the paradox of God's sovereignty and man's responsibility was described as more than amazing, his view *in re* the "well-meaning offer" is characterized as "surpassing strange" (13).

The complainants put it this way:

> In the course of Dr. Clark's examination by Presbytery it became abundantly clear that his rationalism keeps him from doing justice to the precious teaching of Scripture that in the gospel God sincerely offers salvation in Christ to all who hear, reprobate as well as elect, and that he has no pleasure in any one's rejecting this offer but, contrariwise, would have all who hear accept it and be saved [13].

Let us try to define the difference between the complainants and Dr. Clark as sharply as we can.

The difference is not that the complainants insist that the Gospel must be preached to all men promiscuously, while Dr. Clark claims that it must be preached only to the elect. This would be quite impossible, seeing that no preacher is able to single out the elect and separate them from the reprobate in

46

this world. They are agreed that the Gospel must be preached to all men.

Nor is the difference that the complainants openly deny the doctrine of reprobation, while Dr. Clark professes to believe this truth. We read in the *Complaint*: "He believes – as do we all – the doctrine of reprobation" (13).

Again, the difference does not consist in that the complainants characterize the Gospel as an "offer" of Christ or as salvation, while Dr. Clark objects to that term. If the term "offer" is understood in the sense in which it occurs in the confessions, and in which also Calvin uses it (*offere*, from *obfero*, meaning *to present*), there can be no objection to that term, though, to prevent misunderstanding, it would be better to employ the words *to present*, and *presentation*.

Again, even though Dr. Clark objects to the word "sincere" in the sense in which the complainants use that term, afraid to leave the impression that he preaches Arminianism, even this does not touch the real point of difference between them. That God is sincere in the preaching of the Gospel no one would dare to deny. As the complainants rightly ask: "Would it not be blasphemy to deny this?" (13)

But the difference between them does concern *the contents* of the Gospel that must be preached promiscuously to all men.

It is really not a question *to whom* one must preach, or *how* he must preach, but *what* he must preach.

According to the complainants, the preacher is called to proclaim to all his hearers *that God sincerely seeks the salvation of them all.* If this is not their meaning when they write: "in the gospel God sincerely offers salvation in Christ to all who hear, reprobate as well as elect," their words have no meaning at all.

According to Dr. Clark, however, the preacher proclaims to all his hearers promiscuously *that God sincerely seeks the salvation of all the elect.* The elect may be variously named in the preaching: those who repent, they that believe in Christ, that hunger for the bread of life, that thirst for the water of life, that seek, knock, ask, that come to Christ, etc. etc. But they are always the elect.

We may define the issue still more sharply, and limit it to God's intention and attitude in the preaching of the Gospel *with regard to the reprobate.*

For it is more especially about the reprobate and their salvation that the complainants are concerned. Strange though it may seem, paradoxical though it may sound, they want to leave room in their preaching for *the salvation of the reprobate.* For the sake of clarity, therefore, we can safely leave the elect out of our discussion. That God sincerely seeks their salvation is not a matter of controversy. To drag them into the discussion of this question simply confuses things. The question very really concerns the attitude of God with respect to the reprobate. We may limit the controversy to this question: *What must the preacher of the Gospel say of God's intention with respect to the reprobate?* And these, too, may be called by different names, such as, the impenitent, the wicked, the unbelievers, etc.

The answer to this question defines the difference between Dr. Clark and the complainants sharply and precisely.

The complainants answer: The preacher must say that God sincerely seeks the salvation of the reprobate through the preaching of the Gospel.

Dr. Clark answers: That is not true; the preacher may never say that in the name of God.

And, in the light of Scripture, he should say: God seeks his own glory and justification in preparing the reprobate for their just damnation even through the preaching of the Gospel.

That, in thus formulating the difference, I am not doing an injustice to the complainants is very plain from their own words. They say that in the preaching of the Gospel God sincerely offers salvation in Christ to the reprobate, that He has no pleasure in their rejection of the offer, that he would have them, the reprobate, accept the Gospel, and that he would have them be saved. Besides, it is in this sense that they interpret *Ezekiel* 33:11: God has no pleasure in the death of the reprobate, he would have them live; and *2 Peter* 3:9: God does not will that the reprobate should perish, but that they all come to repentance; and *Matthew* 23:37: Christ would have gathered the reprobate under his wings; and *1 Timothy* 2:3, 4: God our Saviour will have all the reprobate to be saved and come unto the knowledge of the truth (13, 14). And it is with the doctrine of universal salvation in mind that they write: "The supreme importance for evangelism of maintaining the Reformed doctrine of the gospel as a universal and sincere offer is self-evident" (14).

Now, you might object, as also Dr. Clark does, that this involves a direct contradiction: God sincerely seeks the salvation of those whom He has from eternity determined not to save. Or: God would have that sinner live whom He does not quicken. Or: God would have the sinner, whom He does not give faith, to accept the gospel. Or: God would have that sinner come to Christ whom He does not draw and who cannot come.

You might object that this is not rational.

But this objection would be of no avail to persuade the complainants of their error. They admit that this is irrational. But they do not want to be rational on this point. In fact, if you should insist on being rational in this respect, they would call you a "rationalist," and at once proceed to seek your expulsion from the church as a dangerous heretic. The whole *Complaint* against Dr. Clark is really concentrated in and based on this one alleged error of his: He claims that the Word of God and the Christian faith are not irrational. According to the complainants, to be reasonable is to be a rationalist. They write that the trouble with Dr. Clark is that

> his rationalism does not permit him to let the two stand unreconciled alongside each other. Rather than do that he would modify the gospel in the interest of reprobation. [This, you understand, is a slanderous remark. – H. H.] Otherwise expressed, he makes the same error as does the Arminian, although he moves in the opposite direction. The Arminian cannot harmonize divine reprobation with the sincere divine offer of salvation to all who hear; hence, he rejects the former. Neither can Dr. Clark harmonize the two, and so he detracts from the latter. Rationalism accounts for both errors [13].

To accuse the complainants of irrationalism is, therefore, of no avail as far as they are concerned. They openly admit – they are even boasting of – their irrational position. To be irrational is, according to them, the glory of a humble, Christian faith.

We shall, therefore, have to prove to them that in their claim that God sincerely seeks the salvation of the reprobate in the preaching of the Gospel, they not only contradict themselves, but they directly contradict Scripture.

And this we hope to do, not because Dr. Clark is in need of our defense, but because we are interested in the pure Reformed truth, and cannot allow it to be camouflaged and corrupted by some self-confessed irrationalists.

But before we proceed to do so, we must prove two things: 1. That the position of the complainants is not irrational as they claim, but involves an Arminian conception of reprobation. 2. That their argumentation on this point in the *Complaint* is very superficial, and characterized by many errors.

In this issue, we will have room to elucidate only point 1.

After all, even though the complainants themselves insist on being irrational, we will have to deal with them according to the rules of logic. If they refuse to be treated rationally, they really forfeit the right to present a complaint to any assembly of normal Christians. And treating them as rational human beings, we must insist that they do not and cannot possibly accept the proposition: God sincerely seeks the salvation of those whom he has sovereignly from eternity determined to be damned.

In other words: I know that they claim to believe this, but I deny their claim; I do not accept it.

Hence, I must try to rationalize their position for them. How can any man, with a show of rationality, insist that God sincerely seeks the salvation of the reprobate? Only when they define *reprobation* as that eternal act of God according to which he determined to damn all those whom he eternally foresaw as rejecting the Gospel.

In other words, I insist that the position of the complainants, as soon as you reject their claim to irrationalism, is purely Arminian.

And their irrationalism is only an attempt to camouflage their real position.

10. Arminianism

The complainants insist that the preacher must proclaim that God sincerely seeks the salvation of the reprobate. And in spite of this ostensibly Arminian position they claim the sole right to the name of being Reformed. This claim they defend by appealing to the principle (?) of irrationality. They take the position that the Reformed faith is irrational. And on that position no one can successfully attack them.

But, as we have seen, if we deny them the right to that irrational position, and, as rational beings, try to explain their position, we discover that they embrace the Arminian view of reprobation.

But let us now also demonstrate how superficial and erroneous this part of the *Complaint* is.

The complainants find it strange that Dr. Clark is reluctant to admit that the Gospel is an offer and an invitation. And they quote from the *Westminster Confession* to condemn this reluctance on the part of Dr. Clark. That *Confession* does not hesitate to speak of the Gospel as an offer, for in VII.3, we read: "Wherein [in the covenant of grace – H.H.] he freely offers unto sinners life and salvation by Jesus Christ."

But how superficial is the reasoning of the complainants here! Dr. Clark is reluctant to speak of the Gospel as an offer and "invitation" in the sense in which the Arminians – and also the complainants – use these terms. They understand these terms as meaning that in the Gospel God sincerely seeks the salvation of the reprobate. But the *Westminster Confession* in the passage quoted knows nothing of this modern connotation of the terms. This should be evident from the fact that the word *offer* is used in the sense of the Latin *offere*, from *obfero*, and may be translated just as well by "present." But that it was far from the minds of the authors of the *Westminster Confession* to teach that in the Gospel God is sincerely seeking the salvation of the reprobate is especially evident from the rest of the same passage: "and promising to give unto all those that are ordained unto life his Holy Spirit, to make them willing and able to believe." This, then, is the promise of the covenant, the promise that must be preached: *God will give to all the elect his Spirit*. But the complainants are not satisfied with this. They insist that Dr. Clark must preach and teach "that in the Gospel God sincerely offers salvation in Christ to all who hear, reprobate as well as elect."

It is, therefore, not strange at all, but quite understandable that Dr. Clark is willing to subscribe to the statement in the *Westminster Confession* to which the complainants refer, while at the same time he is very reluctant to use the terms "offer" and "invitation" when required to do so in the sense of the complainants.

The same superficiality and dodging of the real issue characterizes the following paragraph:

> Dr. Clark steadfastly refuses to describe as sincere the offer which God makes to sinners in the gospel. This is surpassing strange. To be sure, the Westminster standards do not employ the word *sincere* in this connection; but is it not a foregone conclusion that the offer is sincere? Would it not be blasphemy to deny this? For that very reason there was no need of the Westminster divines' describing the gospel offer as sincere. Its sincerity goes without saying. But obviously that is not Dr. Clark's reason for refusing to characterize it as sincere.

No, indeed. Nor would Dr. Clark object to use the word "sincere" to characterize the offer of God as explained in the *Westminster Confession*: God promises to give unto all that are ordained unto life his Holy Spirit. And yet, it is not "surpassing strange" that he refuses to employ that word in the sense in which the complainants would have him use it: that God sincerely offers salvation to the reprobate as well as to elect. And this alone is the issue.

The following interpretation of the Arminian controversy appears to be especially invented to fit the facts in the case of Dr. Clark as the complainants see them:

> When the Arminian controversy was at its height the Reformed churches faced a different situation. It was contended emphatically by the Arminians that the

Reformed doctrine of reprobation rules out the sincerity of God's offer of salvation to the reprobate and that, consequently, the Reformed faith has a gospel only for the elect. Precisely the sincerity of the gospel offer was now at issue [13].

The complainants should not make such broad statements interpreting historical facts without offering definite proof. And where would they find such proof? One would naturally look for it in the *Remonstrantie*, composed by the Arminians in 1610. At that time the "Arminian controversy was at its height." Moreover, in that document the Remonstrants carefully formulated their objections to the Reformed conception of predestination. But in vain does one look for support of the interpretation of their stand offered by the complainants. They simply and openly rejected absolute predestination, both election and reprobation, and instead offered their own, that of election on the ground of foreseen faith and obedience, and of reprobation on the ground of foreseen unbelief and disobedience. They expressly objected to the doctrine (I translate from the Dutch):

> That God – as some say – by an eternal and unchangeable decree ordained some to eternal life, others to eternal damnation, only because of His good pleasure, without regard to their righteousness or disobedience. That further in virtue of a second decree the elect must necessarily and inevitably be saved and cannot be lost, and the reprobate – constituting by far the larger part – must necessarily and inevitably be damned.

They could not accept the doctrine:

> "That Jesus Christ did not die for all men, but only for the elect"; and that in the elect "the Holy Spirit operated with irresistible power, so that they must be converted

and believe and thus necessarily be saved, while the reprobate do not receive this grace."

They did, indeed, point to the inconsistency that the reprobate, according to the revealed will of God, are also called to conversion and faith, but that they rationalistically concluded from this external calling to a denial of reprobation, as the complainants interpret – of this one does not find a trace in the *Remonstrantie*.

It would seem, therefore, that they simply impose their own interpretation upon the history of the Arminian controversy, in order to show that Dr. Clark, by a similar, rationalistic error, moves in the opposite direction, and denies the sincere offer of salvation on the part of God to the reprobate. This is superficial because it falsely interprets the facts.

Superficial, too, and erroneous, is the quotation the complainants offer from the Canons, and the argument based on this erroneous quotation. The quotation as it appears in the *Complaint* is as follows:

> As many as are called by the gospel, are unfeignedly called. For God hath most earnestly and truly declared in His Word what will be acceptable to him; namely, that all who are called should comply with the invitation (Third and Fourth Heads of Doctrine, art. 8).

And the argument the complainants base on this quotation is as follows:

> In the course of his examination Dr. Clark did indeed express agreement with this teaching of Dort, but he made it clear that in doing so he conceived of the gospel as a command.... He said that it is the preceptive will of God that those who hear shall believe the gospel, and it is "acceptable" to God that they do so because he insists on being obeyed. But the Synod of Dort obviously meant

much more than that when it employed the word "accept-able." That appears from its description of the gospel as an invitation, from its insistence that all who are called are called "unfeignedly," as well as from the fact that it was refuting the Arminian contention that the Reformed faith leaves no room for a sincere offer of salvation made by God to the reprobate. What the authors of the Canons had in mind was that God has "no pleasure in the death of the wicked, but that the wicked turn from his way and live" [*Ezekiel* 33:11].

Now, we do not have to defend Dr. Clark's position that the gospel is a command. This is not the point we wish to make. Nor is it our purpose at present to refute the interpretation the complainants give to this passage of the Canons, though it may be remarked that on the face of the matter it seems very farfetched. Surely, if it had been the intention of the fathers of Dordt to express that God sincerely seeks the salvation of the reprobate, they could have chosen less ambiguous words.

But the point we do wish to make is that the complainants very superficially quote a wrong translation, arrive at the conclusion that the Canons characterize the Gospel as an invitation, and make this error the basis of their argument against Dr. Clark's refusal to call the Gospel by that name.

If laymen, who have access only to existing translations, make such errors, it is excusable. But that men of learning – who are able to consult the Latin original, and, besides, are acquainted with the Holland translation of the Canons – make such blunders is not to be excused. When they, nevertheless, do meet their opponents with such erroneous arguments, they give evidence of having done very superficial and careless work.

Fact is that the Canons, in the passage quoted, do not describe the Gospel as an invitation at all. The Latin original is as follows: "Serio enim et verissime ostendit Deus verbo suo, quid sibi gratum sit, nimirum, ut vocati ad se veniant." That is: "God seriously and truly declares in His Word what is pleasing to him, namely, that the called come unto him." And this is correctly rendered in the Dutch translation: "Want God betoont ernstiglijk and waarachtiglijk in Zijn Woord, wat Hem aangenaam is; namelijk, dat de geroepen tot Hem komen."

The passage, therefore, does not describe the Gospel as an invitation. And the argument that is based on this wrong translation must fall together with the translation.

As far as this passage of the Canons is concerned, Dr. Clark does not have to call the Gospel an invitation and retains the right to his interpretation that it is a command, and that the command obeyed is pleasing to God, because it is pleasing to him that men glorify him. This interpretation is given of the eighth article of the Canons, III, IV, more than once. (See, for example, Ds. T. Bos, *De Dordtsche Leerregelen*, page 155.)

But whether this is the correct interpretation of the passage or not, the complainants should not make the blunder of basing an argument on an erroneous translation.

11. Saving the Reprobate

Superficial, too, is the way in which the *Complaint* makes use of quotations from Calvin to prove that the great Reformer supports its contention that God earnestly seeks the salvation of all men, reprobate as well as elect.

The complainants quote Calvin on the well-known text in *Ezekiel* 18:28, and their quotation appears to justify their contention only when you read it very superficially, and especially when you permit it to stand out of its proper context. Yet, even the quotation does not teach that "God sincerely offers salvation to all who hear, reprobate as well as elect, and that He has no pleasure in any one's rejecting this offer but, contrariwise, would have all who hear accept it and be saved," as the complainants contend. When Calvin writes "that God wills not the death of a sinner, because he meets him on his own accord, and is not only prepared to receive all who fly to his pity, but he calls them to him with a loud voice, when he sees how they are alienated from all hope of safety," he does not teach that God is ready to receive the reprobate, since they do not belong to those "who fly to his pity." But this becomes much clearer in what Calvin continues to write in explanation of the same text. We quote:

> God is said *not to wish the death of a sinner.* How so? Since he wishes all to be converted. Now we must see how God wishes all to be converted; for repentance is surely his peculiar gift: As it is his office to create men, so it is his province to renew them, and restore his image within them. For this reason we are said to be his workmanship, that is, his fashioning (*Ephesians* 2:10). Since, therefore, repentance is a kind of second creation, it follows that it is not in man's power; and if it is equally in God's power to convert men as well as to create them, it follows that the reprobate are not converted, because God does not wish their conversion; for if he wished it, he could do it; and hence it appears that he does not wish it. But again they argue foolishly: Since God does not wish all to be converted, he is himself deceptive, and nothing can be certainly stated concerning his paternal benevolence. But this knot is easily untied, for he does not leave us in suspense when he says that he wishes all to be saved. Why so? For if no one repents without finding God propitious, then his sentence is filled up. But we must remark that he puts on a twofold character, for he here wishes to be taken at his word. As I have already said, the Prophet does not here dispute with subtlety about his

incomprehensible plans, but wishes to keep our attention close to God's Word. Now, what are the contents of
this Word? The law, the prophets, and the gospel. Now
all are called to repentance, and the hope of salvation
is promised them when they repent: This is true since
God rejects no returning sinner: He pardons all without
exception; meanwhile, this will of God which he sets
forth in his Word does not prevent him from decreeing
before the world was created what he would do with
every individual, and as I have now said, the Prophet
only shows here, that when we have been converted we
need not doubt that God immediately meets us and
shows himself propitious.

Now, the complainants would, most probably, accuse Calvin of rationalism since he here unties a knot, the very knot
which they claim cannot be untied. He explains in what sense
God can invite all men to salvation though he does not wish
all men to be saved. His answer is that in this passage from
Ezekiel he promises salvation only to those that are converted
and repent, and that, since the work of conversion and repentance is his creation, he, therefore, really promises salvation
only to the elect. And thus it is evident that Calvin, in this
passage from his *Commentaries*, never taught the doctrine of
the complainants, that God sincerely desires reprobate as well
as elect to be saved.

That this is, indeed, the interpretation of this text as Calvin
would give it is still more clearly evident from what we find
in *Calvin's Calvinism*, pages 99-100. We quote:

All this Pighius loudly denies, adducing that passage
of the apostle (*1 Timothy* 2:4): "Who will have all men
to be saved"; and referring to *Ezekiel* 18:23, he argues
thus: "That God wills not the death of a sinner may be
taken upon his oath, where he says by that prophet: As I

live, says the Lord, I have no pleasure in the death of the wicked that dies, but rather that he should return from his ways and live." Now we reply, that as the language of the prophet here is an exhortation to repentance, it is not at all marvelous in him to declare that he wills all men to be saved. For the mutual relation between threats and promises shows that such forms of speaking are *conditional.* In this same manner God declared to the Ninevites, and to the kings of Gerar and Egypt, that He would do that which in reality He did not intend to do, for their repentance averted the punishment which He had threatened to inflict upon them. Whence it is evident that the punishment was announced on condition of their remaining obstinate and impenitent. And yet, the denunciation of punishment was positive, as if it had been an irrevocable decree. But after God had terrified them with the apprehension of His wrath, and had fully humbled them as not being utterly desperate, He encouraged them with the hope of pardon, that they might feel that there was yet left open a space for remedy. Just so it is with the *conditional promises* of God which invite all men to salvation. They do not positively prove that which God has decreed in His counsel, but declare only that which God is ready to do to all those that are brought to faith and repentance.

But men untaught of God, not understanding these things, allege that we here attribute to God a twofold or double will. Whereas God is so far from being variable, that no shadow of such variableness appertains to Him, even in the most remote degree. Hence, Pighius, ignorant of the divine nature of these things, thus argues: "What else is this but making of God the mocker of men, if God is represented as really not willing that which He professes to will, and as not having pleasure in that which in reality He has pleasure?" But if these two members of

the sentence be read in conjunction, as they ought to be
– "I have no pleasure in the death of the wicked"; and:
"But that the wicked turn from his way and live" – read
these two propositions in connection with each other,
and the calumny is washed off at once. God requires of
us this conversion or "turning away from our iniquity,"
and in whomsoever He finds it He disappoints not such
a one of the promised reward of eternal life. Wherefore,
God is as much said to have pleasure in, and to will, this
eternal life, as to have pleasure in the repentance; and
He has pleasure in the repentance, because He invites
all men to it by His Word. Now all this is in perfect harmony with His secret and eternal counsel, by which He
decreed to convert none but His own elect. None but
God's elect, therefore, ever turn from their wickedness.
And yet, the adorable God is not, on these accounts, to
be considered variable or capable of change, because
as a Lawgiver He enlightens all men with the external
doctrine of *conditional life*. In this primary sense He calls
or invites *all men* to eternal life. But in the latter case, He
brings to eternal life those whom He willed according
to His eternal purpose, regenerating by His Spirit, as an
eternal Father, His own children only.

Now, let the complainants admit that if Dr. Clark had written the above, they would immediately characterize it as a bit
of rationalism. For Calvin here harmonizes *Ezekiel* 18:23 with
God's eternal counsel of election and reprobation, and that,
too, in such a way that he explains the former in the light of
the latter. When he explains that in such passages as *Ezekiel*
18:23 God promises conditional life to all, he evidently means
that through the Gospel God declares that he will give life to all
that repent. And since it is God who must give repentance, in
reality he promises life only to the elect, and to none other.

Surely, the complainants will have to admit that this differs radically from their view that God sincerely seeks the salvation of all men – the reprobate as well as the elect.

What the Reformer here teaches is that although the preaching of the Gospel by men is general and promiscuous, the content is always particular. God saves those that fly to him for pity and redemption, that come to him, that forsake their wicked ways, repent, and believe.

And this "condition" of salvation not one man is able to fulfill of himself. God fulfills his own condition. He gives grace to repent, to believe, to come to him.

That is Reformed theology. To say that God sincerely seeks the salvation of all that hear the Gospel, as the complainants would have the preacher of the Gospel proclaim, is Arminian pure and simple.

And if they quote Calvin, they should quote him fully, lest they ascribe to that Reformer teachings which he always abhorred.

We have more to say on this subject, but this must wait till our next issue, the Lord willing.

12. John Calvin

How superficially they quote Calvin who try to make him say, as do the complainants, that God sincerely seeks and wills the salvation of all men; or that Scripture teaches the contradiction that on the one hand God wills that all men shall be saved, and on the other hand wills the salvation of the elect, is evident to all that are acquainted with the works of the Reformer.

Fact is, and the fact is striking indeed, that the very same passages from Holy Writ to which the complainants appeal in support of their position that God sincerely seeks the salvation of all men, were quoted against Calvin by the opponents of his doctrine of predestination and particular grace, as they were quoted against Augustine before him.

But Calvin does not admit that these passages teach a certain general grace, nor that they contradict or even apparently contradict the current teaching of the Bible that God saves and wills to save only the elect. On the contrary, he always seeks to explain them in the light of the doctrine of predestination and to show that they are in harmony with this doctrine.

Defending the doctrine of sovereign reprobation, Calvin explains some of these texts which the opponents of this doctrine are wont to quote to disprove it. Writes he, *Institutes* III.24.15 (we translate from the Latin):

> But since a few passages of Scripture are wont to be adduced in which God seems to deny that it is caused by his ordinance that the wicked perish, except in so far that, ignoring his loud calling, they willingly procure death unto themselves, let us by explaining these texts briefly demonstrate that they do not stand in opposition to the sentiments expressed above [*i.e.*, concerning reprobation – H.H.]. The place in *Ezekiel* is adduced, where it is said that God does not desire [will, *nolit*] the death of the wicked, but rather that he should turn and live. If one will extend this to the whole human race, what may be the reason why he does not stir up to repentance many whose minds are more flexible to obedience than of those who harden themselves more and more against his repeated invitations? According to Christ's own testimony, the preaching of the gospel and the miracles would have produced more fruit with the Ninevites and Sodomites than in Judea. How come, then, if God wills all to be saved, that he does not open the door of repentance to those wretched ones that would be more ready to receive his grace? From this we see that this place is violently

distorted if the will of God of which the prophet speaks is presented as opposed to his eternal counsel by which he distinguished the elect from the reprobate. Now if one asks, what is the true meaning of the prophet, the answer is that he only would give to those that repent the hope of forgiveness. And this is the brief content, that it must not be doubted that God is ready to forgive as soon as the sinner is converted. Hence, he does not wish his death in so far as he does want his repentance. Experience, however, teaches that he so wills the repentance of those whom he calls to him that he does not touch the hearts of all. Nevertheless, it must not be said that he deals falsely, for even though the external voice only renders inexcusable those that hear it, it is nevertheless truly considered a testimony of the grace of God, whereby men are reconciled to him. Let us, therefore, hold to the true sense of the prophet, that God does not desire the death of the sinner: that the godly may trust that as soon as they have been touched with conversion, pardon is prepared for them with God, and that the wicked may understand that they double their iniquity because they do not respond to so great a clemency and readiness of God. Penitence therefore always meets with the mercy of God: but who they are upon whom penitence is bestowed is clearly set forth by all the prophets and apostles, and even by Ezekiel himself.

Now, the complainants are bound to accuse Calvin of rationalism here. If they will but be consistent, and treat Calvin as they do Dr. Clark, they will accuse the Reformer of explaining *Ezekiel* 18:23 "in favor of reprobation." For it is precisely his avowed purpose in the above paragraph so to explain this passage that it does not contradict the truth concerning the decree of reprobation. According to Calvin, it does not contradict or stand opposed to reprobation at all (*nihil...adversari*).

And it is very evident that his explanation of the text means briefly that God does not will the death of the elect, since he does not desire the death of the sinner in the same sense as he does will his conversion, and since he bestows conversion only on the elect.

Two things should be evident: 1. Calvin has no sympathy with the basic position of the complainants that there are contradictions in Scripture which no one should attempt to explain; and 2. he does explain those passages of Scripture that appear to speak of a willingness on the part of God to save all men in such a way as to bring them in harmony with his eternal counsel of predestination.

If the complainants had shown the same regard for Dr. Clark as they like to show to Calvin, they would never have written their complaint.

Anyone that is acquainted with Calvin's *Institutes* knows that the passage we quoted is no isolated example of the Reformer's method. In III. 24. 16 he applies the same method of exegesis to *1 Timothy* 2:4. We must note, says he, that the apostle in this passage combines two things: that God wills all men to be saved, and that he would have them all come to knowledge of the truth. But, he asks, if you insist that it be firmly decreed in God's counsel that all shall receive the doctrine of salvation, how can Moses address the children of Israel as follows: "For what nation is there so glorious that God approaches to it as to thee?" (Quae gens est tam inclyta, ut ad eam appropinquet Deus sicut ad te?) "How has it come to pass," thus he continues, "that God has deprived many peoples of the light of the gospel, which others enjoy?" It is evident, then, that God does not want all men to come to the knowledge of the truth, and that it follows that he does not will all men to be saved. And then he continues to explain the text as having reference to different ranks and classes of men.

Pure rationalism, the complainants would call this, if it were not Calvin that wrote it.

Even the text from 2 *Peter* 3:9, on which the complainants quote Calvin from another source, is explained in a similar way in the *Institutes* (III. 24. 17). He admits that the opponents seem to have more reason on their side when they quote this text to prove that God wills all men to be saved. But he nevertheless "unties this knot at once" by calling attention to the second part of the text stating that God wills that all men should come to repentance. For, he argues, by this will of God to receive unto repentance none other can be understood than that which is taught everywhere in Scripture (quia voluntas recipiendi ad poententiam non alia intelligi potest nisi quae passim traditur). And then he argues that conversion is in the hand of God, and it is proper to ask him whether he will convert all men. But since it is evident that he does not will to convert all men, it is equally evident that he does not will that all men be saved, and that the text in 2 *Peter* 3:9 teaches only that God wills that those be saved whom he brings to repentance.

Rationalism?

That it is will have to be the judgment of the complainants.

But all sound, Reformed theologians and exegetes have always insisted that Scripture must be explained in its own light and that difficult passages must be explained in harmony with the current teaching of the Bible.

The position of the complainants is decidedly not Calvinistic. They are trying to oust Calvin, just as their Christian Reformed brethren did in 1924.

And why did they select one passage from Calvin in which he explains 2 *Peter* 3:9 in a way that might seem to favor their position somewhat? Why did they not also quote from the *Institutes*? Or from *Calvin's Calvinism*?

Or why did they not quote what Dr. A. Kuyper, Sr., has to say on the same text? Surely, him too they honor as a Calvinist. And they cannot have been ignorant of the explanation he offers of the same passage in *Peter*. In his "Dat de genade particulier is," he argues that the text in *2 Peter* 3:9 cannot possibly mean that God desires the salvation of all men, for the simple reason that in that case it would also teach that Christ would never come and that the salvation for which the people of God long would be postponed indefinitely. Hence, he concludes, the text must mean that God is longsuffering over His people, not willing that any of them should be lost, but that all should come to repentance. But why, if it was the purpose of the complainants to give a fair picture of the opinion of Reformed theologians, did they not also quote what Dr. Kuyper has to say on this passage from *Second Peter*?

To say the least, they now leave the impression of having done very superficial work, unworthy of theologians.

And this, too, requires an explanation: Why do they always quote texts, and show a special preference for them, which opponents of the doctrine of the truth of sovereign grace have always used in the same way and for the same purpose as they, the complainants, do?

Ex ungue leonem!

13. Calvin on Common Grace

The *Complaint* quotes a long list of references to passages in the *Gospel according to John*, in which, according to Dr. Herman Kuiper, from whose book on *Calvin on Common Grace* the list is obtained, Calvin finds "the idea that God invites both elect and reprobate men to salvation and offers salvation to all men promiscuously."

We have neither the space nor the desire to check up on

67

this list of texts. One or two remarks may suffice in this connection.

First of all, for my own satisfaction I did look up half a dozen of the references quoted, and discovered that many of them have nothing whatever to do with the question under discussion. Thus, for instance, one of the references is *John 1:6*. The text reads: "There was a man sent from God, whose name was John." Curious how Calvin could discover in this passage "the idea that God invites both elect and reprobate men to salvation and offers salvation to all men promiscuously," we looked up the Reformer's commentary on the text, and found nothing that even approaches the above mentioned idea. Nor did we find anything on some of the other passages referred to.

Secondly, I consider the conclusion arrived at by the author of *Calvin on Common Grace*, and quoted by the complainants with evident approval, very superficial. That conclusion reads as follows:

> We may as well try to budge a mountain of solid granite with our finger as endeavor to harmonize these declarations....
>
> Must we then conclude that Calvin taught that God has a double will and is at variance with Himself? Our author expressly declares that he emphatically repudiates the view that God has more than one will. He explicitly teaches that we must not think that God has a double will. God does not in Himself will opposites. But it is impossible for us to comprehend and fathom the Most High. To our apprehension the will of God is manifold. As far as we can see, God does will what seems to be opposed to His will....
>
> In short, Calvin makes it plain that in his view the paradoxes which we have just reviewed are paradoxes involved in the teaching of Holy Scripture itself.

Now, it is indeed true that one may select a list of passages in the voluminous writings of Calvin that would seem to corroborate the view expressed above. And this need not surprise us. In his relatively short life Calvin wrote many books. He was a prolific writer. From the time he began to write his *Institutes*, when he was only twenty-four years old, until his death, he wrote almost incessantly. It need not surprise us, then, that if one peruses Calvin's works superficially, with the purpose in mind to prove that he taught that God earnestly seeks the salvation of the reprobate, and that there are contradictions in Scripture, he will find what he is looking for in the first place. It would not be difficult, according to this superficial method of studying, to demonstrate that Augustine did not believe in absolute predestination, or that Dr. A. Kuyper was a Hegelian pantheist.

Fact is, however, that one may also find many passages in the works of Calvin in which he explains those texts of Holy Writ that appear to teach God's saving love for all men, and explains them in the light of the doctrine of predestination, particularly of reprobation. In other words, those passages of his writings in which he seems to be satisfied to let the paradox stand, the apparent contradictions unexplained, are not his last word.

That this is true, we have already abundantly proved by quotations from his writings. It was especially when the opponent of the truth of predestination attacked his position that the Reformer set himself to explain the texts adduced by those opponents, and which seemingly teach that God wills the salvation of all men.

What else could he do?

Or what else would you expect any truly Reformed man to do? Always these opponents fling the same texts in the face of those that uphold the doctrine of absolute predestination.

And let it be a warning that these texts are the very same that are now appealed to by the complainants. They are in bad company. They, *i.e.*, the opponents of the truth of God's sovereign predestination, made use of such texts as *Matthew 23:37, 1 Timothy 2:4, 2 Peter 3:9, etc.* to oppose Augustine, to gainsay Calvin, to refute Gomarus and the fathers of Dordt, to contradict Dr. A. Kuyper, Sr., when he began to take a stand for the Reformed truth of predestination.

And what did all these men do?

Did they admit that these passages from Scripture actually taught what the opponents made them say? Did they seek an easy refuge in the doctrine of contradictions?

They most emphatically did not.

On the contrary, one and all they explained those passages of Scripture and harmonized them with the truth of sovereign election and reprobation.

So did Augustine.

And Calvin followed him, as is well known, and did the same thing.

Let me adduce just one or two more quotations from Calvin to prove this statement.

When Pighius opposes the truth by appealing to *Psalm* 145:9 (a text also quoted by the Christian Reformed Synod of 1924), the Reformer replies:

> Let our readers hence gather how much religion and conscience Pighius has in dealing with Holy Scripture! He then adds from the *Psalm*, "The Lord is good to all" (145:9), from which he concludes that *therefore* all were ordained to eternal life. Now, if this be true, the kingdom of Heaven is open for dogs and asses! For the Psalmist is not magnifying that goodness of God only which he shows to man, but that also which He shows to all His works. But why should not Pighius thus fight for his brethren? [*Calvin's Calvinism*, 88].

The next Scripture which he tacks on to his argument is that of Paul, who declares (he says) that God "included all under sin, that He might have mercy upon all" (*Romans* 11:32). As if Paul in this passage were disputing about the *number* of men! Whereas he is abstractedly lauding the grace of God toward *all* of *us* who attain unto salvation. Most certainly nothing was less in the mind of the apostle than an extension of the mercy of God to all men. His sole object was to prostrate all glorying of the flesh, that we may clearly understand that no man will ever be saved but he whom God saved by grace alone. Behold, then, with what glorious arguments our opponent demonstrates that none is chosen unto salvation from above in preference to others! And yet this ape of Euclid puffs himself off in the titles of all his chapters as a reasoner [89].

When Pighius refers to the text in 1 *Timothy* 4:2, giving it the same interpretation the complainants prefer, Calvin answers, first of all:

The difficulty…is solved in one moment, and by one question, namely, *How* does God wish all men to come to the knowledge of the truth? For Paul couples this *salvation* and this *coming to the knowledge of the truth* together. Now, I would ask, did the same will of God stand the same from the beginning of the world or not? For if God willed or wished that His truth should be known unto *all men*, how was it that He did not proclaim and make known His law to the Gentiles also? Why did He confine the light within the narrow limits of Judea?

And this part of the argument the Reformer concludes as follows:

Now let Pighius boast, if he can, that God wills *all men* to be saved! The above arguments, founded on the Scriptures, prove that even the external preaching of the doctrine of salvation, which is far inferior to the illumination of the Spirit, was not made common to *all men* [103, 104].

And he continues to explain:

> The knot immediately before us is not yet, I confess, untied. I have nevertheless extorted from Pighius thus much: that no one but a man deprived of his common sense and common knowledge can believe that salvation was ordained by the secret counsel of God equally and indiscriminately for all men. The true meaning of Paul, however, in the passage now under consideration is perfectly clear and intelligible to every one who is not determined on contention. The apostle is exhorting that all solemn "supplications, prayers, intercessions, and giving of thanks, be made for all men: for kings and all that are in authority." And because there were, in that age, so many and such wrathful and bitter enemies of the Church, Paul, to prevent despair from hindering the prayers of the faithful, hastens to meet their distresses by earnestly entreating them to be instant in prayer "for all men," and especially for "all those in authority." "For [says the apostle] God will have *all men* to be saved." Who does not see that the apostle is here speaking of *orders of men* rather than of individuals? [105].

How superficial and misleading is the conclusion of the author of *Calvin on Common Grace* when he insists that Calvin is satisfied with paradoxes!

And how different is the Reformer's attitude, his position with regard to the question under consideration, from that of the complainants, who rather explain *1 Timothy* 2:4 as meaning that God sincerely offers salvation to those whom he has predetermined to leave to the just recompense of their sins, and that he is a benevolent being that delights not in the suffering of his creatures, *etc.* Compare *The Text of a Complaint*, page 14.

14. Contradicting Scripture

With reference to the last point of the *Complaint*, I have demonstrated thus far, first of all, that the claim on the part of the complainants to the right of an irrational position must be denied them: Their position, that God seeks sincerely the salvation of the reprobate is not irrational, but presupposes an Arminian view of reprobation; and, secondly, that their argument in support of this their contention is very superficial throughout.

The last point I wish to make in this connection is that, in their claim that God seeks the salvation of the reprobate, they directly contradict Holy Writ.

In support of this statement, I might take the general observation, frequently made by Calvin, that it is not God's good pleasure that the Gospel be preached to all men, or even to the majority of men. This is simply a fact, but this is also plainly expressed in Scripture, and it is pointed out in our confessions. A fact it is, for in the old dispensation the Gospel was revealed, for many a century, only to one nation; and at the beginning of the new dispensation the preaching of the Gospel was entrusted to only a few men, so that it must necessarily require many years before the tidings of salvation could reach every nation. And Israel is more than once reminded of this distinction, as, for instance, in *Psalm* 147:19-20: "He shows his word unto Jacob, his statutes and his judgments unto Israel. He has not dealt so with any nation: and as for his judgments, they have not known them. Praise the Lord." And the Canons of Dordrecht, 11, 5, declare that the promise of the Gospel "ought to be declared and published to all nations, and to all persons promiscuously and without distinction, *to whom God out of his good pleasure sends the gospel.*" Now, if the preaching of the Gospel is strictly under the direction of God's pleasure, and if, according to that good pleasure, the Gospel was sent to only a comparatively small number of men, what becomes of this earnest desire on the part of God to save the reprobate?

But I will remark this only in passing. The complainants might object that they do not claim that God sincerely seeks the salvation of all the reprobate, but only of those that hear the Gospel. I will, therefore, conclusively prove to them from Scripture that by this claim they contradict, not themselves, for this they admit, but Holy Scripture itself. And I will do so by quoting a few passages from Holy Writ that leave no doubt as to their meaning.

Turn to the sixth chapter from the prophecy of *Isaiah*. It speaks of Isaiah's calling to preach. And what is his very special commission? You find it in the following words:

> Go, and tell this people. Hear indeed, but understand not; and see indeed, but perceive not. Make the heart of this people fat, and make their ears heavy, and shut their eyes; lest they see with their eyes, and hear with their ears, and understand with their hearts, and convert, and be healed [9-10].

Let the complainants admit that Isaiah is called to preach the Gospel to Israel, and that through this preaching the remnant according to the election of grace will be saved. And let them also admit that, according to the good pleasure of God, this same preaching must serve to the hardening and damnation of the reprobate. They will have to admit this, for the text allows of no other interpretation. And admitting this, they will have to confess that their claim that God through the preaching of the Gospel sincerely seeks the salvation of the reprobate stands in flat contradiction with the Word of God.

If there should be any doubt in their minds as to the meaning of the above passage from *Isaiah*, let them turn to *John* 12:37*ff.* where we read:

> But though he had done many miracles before them, yet they believed not on him, that the saying of Esaias the prophet might be fulfilled, which he spoke: Lord, who has believed our report? and to whom has the arm of the Lord been revealed? Therefore they *could not* believe, because that Esaias said again, He has blinded their eyes, and hardened their heart; that they should not see with their eyes, nor understand with their heart, and be converted, and I should heal them.

What, in the light of these passages, becomes of the vain theory that God, in the preaching of the Gospel, sincerely seeks the salvation of the reprobate, as the complainants claim?

Or again, consider the explanation the Lord Jesus Himself offers to His disciples of the fact that He speaks to the people in parables:

> And he said unto them, Unto you it is given to know the mystery of the kingdom of God: but unto them that are without, all these things are done in parables: That seeing they may see, and not perceive; and hearing they may hear, and not understand; lest at any time they should be converted, and their sins may be forgiven them.

Note here: 1. That under the preaching of the Gospel *it is given* to the elect to know the mystery of the kingdom of heaven. 2. That they that are without are the reprobate. 3. That before their eyes the things of the kingdom of God *are done* in parables: Every time a sower goes forth to sow, he enacts a thing of the kingdom of God in parable. 4. That the Lord points to these enacted parables by his teaching. 5. That this is done, not to seek the salvation of the reprobate, but that they may emphatically see and hear (*seeing see*, and *hearing hear*) with their natural perception, without spiritually understanding these things. 6. And, finally, that the purpose is expressed in the words: "Lest they should be converted, and their sins should be forgiven them."

Passages like the above (and we will quote more) plainly teach that it is God's good pleasure, not to save, but to harden the reprobate by the preaching of the Gospel.

The complainants contradict Scripture.

15. An Arminian Gospel

If I should refer to all the passages of Holy Writ that prove that the complainants contradict Scripture when they insist that God sincerely seeks the salvation of the reprobate through the preaching of the Gospel, this discussion would become practically endless.

And I intend to conclude it in this article.

Hence, I will make just a few selections, in order that it may become abundantly evident that my position is not based on human reason, but on the revelation of God in the Holy Scriptures.

Let us attend to *Matthew* 11:25-27, the context of that well known passage: "Come unto me, all you that labor and are heavy laden, and I will give you rest." We read there:

> At that time Jesus answered and said, I thank you, O Father, Lord of Heaven and Earth, because you have hid these things from the wise and prudent, and have revealed them unto babes. Even so, Father: for so it seemed good in your sight. All things are delivered unto me of my Father; and no man knows the Son, but the

Father; neither knows any man the Father, save the Son,
and he to whomsoever the Father will reveal him.

Let us, in connection with this passage, briefly notice the
following points of importance:

1. That Jesus here *answered*. Answered whom? Evidently,
the Father. But to what do his words and thanksgiving here
contain an answer? To something the Father had done, and
that, too, through the preaching and labors of our Saviour.
This is evident from the context. While the Lord preached
the Gospel of the kingdom and performed his mighty works,
a two-fold effect had become evident.

There were the mighty, who always took the kingdom of
God by force, whether it was John or Jesus that preached its
Gospel; and there were the miserable men of that genera-
tion, whom Jesus compares to the children in the market,
calling unto their fellows: "We have piped unto you, and
you have not danced; we have mourned unto you, and you
have not lamented." Never did they enter the kingdom of
Heaven. John preached it, but they said that he had a devil,
because he came neither eating nor drinking; Jesus came
eating and drinking, and they called him a glutton and
winebibber. To John they piped, and he would not dance;
hence, they must have nothing of his Gospel. Before Jesus
they lamented, and he would not mourn; and, therefore,
they rejected his Gospel. And in connection with this latter
effect of his preaching, the Lord upbraids the cities, "wherein
most of his mighty works were done, because they repented
not" (20). A twofold effect, therefore, had become manifest
under the same preaching.

2. That Jesus ascribes this twofold effect to the work of the
Father. He is the Lord of Heaven and Earth, sovereign also with
respect to the work of salvation. The preaching of the Gospel

becomes effective only through his power and operation. And that operation is twofold: He hides the things of the kingdom of God, and he reveals them.

3. That all this is quite in harmony with the truth, that no man knows the Son, but the Father; and that no one can know the Father, but the Son, and he to whom the Son will reveal him.

4. That the ultimate reason and cause of this operation of the Father, according to which, even under the preaching of the Gospel, he hides and reveals, is the good pleasure of God: "Even so, Father, for so it seemed good in your sight."

Now let the complainants make plain that they do not flatly contradict these words of Jesus when they insist that God sincerely seeks the salvation of the reprobate through the preaching of the Gospel.

May I, further, just remind the complainants of the passage in *Romans* 9:1-18? And let it suffice to point out the main line of the apostle's argument. He explains the fact that many Israelites had not obtained salvation, while the remnant obtained it, from the sovereign purpose of God concerning election and reprobation. The Word of God had not become of none effect, even though many Israelites were not saved, for only the children of the promise are counted for the seed. And there are the elect in distinction from the reprobate, Jacob in distinction from Esau. Even in relation to Israel as a nation God remains sovereign to save whom he will: "I will have mercy on whom I will have mercy, and I will have compassion on whom I will have compassion" (15). And, after he referred to God's sovereign dealings with Pharaoh, he concludes this section with the words: "Therefore he has mercy on whom he will have mercy, and whom he will he hardens."

I would very much like to see the complainants explain this passage in such a way that it becomes plain that they do not openly contradict the Scriptures when they hold that God sincerely seeks the salvation of the reprobate.

One more passage, 2 *Corinthians* 2:14-16:

> Now thanks be unto God, who always causes us to triumph, and makes manifest the savor of Christ in them that are saved and in them that perish: To the one we are a savor of death unto death; and to the other the savor of life unto life. And who is sufficient unto these things?

The point here is: 1. That the apostles, in their preaching of the Gospel, are both a savor of death unto death, and a savor of life unto life. And 2. That in both cases they are a sweet savor of Christ unto God. And the preacher of the Gospel that is not willing to be such a sweet savor unto God in them that are saved and in them that perish simply cannot be a minister of the Word of God.

But what then?

What becomes of the contention of the complainants that God sincerely seeks the salvation of all men, the reprobate included, through the preaching of the Gospel?

And what to think of their final statement: "The supreme importance for evangelism of maintaining the Reformed doctrine of the Gospel as a universal and sincere offer of salvation is self-evident"?

Do they, in this statement, not reveal their real intention? They first claimed that the Reformed doctrine of the Gospel honors the paradox, the contradiction: God wills to save all men; he wills to save only the elect. Must they, then, not preach that paradox, if they would proclaim the full Gospel, according to their own contention? Must they not do justice to that Gospel, and hide nothing of it, whether in "evangelistic" work or in the ministry of the Word in the Church?

But no; here they tacitly admit that, for evangelistic purposes, their paradoxical Gospel is not suitable. And so they propose to forget the one side of their paradox, and to present the Gospel only as a "universal and sincere offer of salvation." And that means that they intend to limit themselves to the proclamation that God sincerely seeks the salvation of all men.

In practice, they intend to preach an Arminian gospel.

They are afraid of their own paradox.

16. Presbytery Minutes

Both because the discussion is interesting in itself, and because we are discussing the case of Dr. Clark in our paper, our readers may be interested in the following report, which we reprint from *The Presbyterian Guardian* of April 10, 1945:

> The Presbytery of Philadelphia of The Orthodox Presbyterian Church held its regular spring meeting on March 19th in Mediator Church, Philadelphia. The principal item of business was the consideration of the proposed *Answer* to the *Complaint* against the actions of the presbytery relative to the licensure and ordination of the Rev. Gordon H. Clark, Ph. D. Discussion of the Clark case lasted for ten hours without reaching any final conclusion of the matter, and presbytery adjourned at midnight to reconvene ten days later.
>
> The devotional hour was led by the Rev. Glenn R. Coie, pastor of Knox Church, Silver Spring, Md., and the subject of his meditation was "Holy Boldness."
>
> The presbytery was called to order at 11:30 and constituted with prayer by the Rev. Edward L. Kellogg, moderator. Following the reading of communications, and after lengthy discussion of the docket, the presbytery placed only two matters ahead of consideration of the Clark case. A pastoral call from Faith Church, Lincoln, Nebr., which had been referred from the Presbytery of

the Dakotas, was placed in the hands of licentiate Delbert Schowalter, and an Auditing Committee was appointed. After disposal of these two matters, the presbytery recessed for lunch.

Corresponding members who were seated by the presbytery included Mr. Mark Fakkema, general secretary of the National Union of Christian Schools and an elder of the Christian Reformed Church, and all ministers and elders of other presbyteries of The Orthodox Presbyterian Church, of whom there were a great many in attendance.

Ruling Elder Alan Tichenor, chairman of the committee elected to answer the *Complaint*, gave a brief report of the committee's work. The *Answer* was not presented for action but was filed with the clerk. It was merely stated that the committee had prepared an answer, printed two hundred copies, and distributed one hundred twenty-five, leaving seventy-five still available. Thus the report which takes the form of a reply of the presbytery, and is introduced as an answer proposed to the presbytery by the committee, was not actually proposed to the presbytery as presbytery's answer to the *Complaint*. Immediately after this brief report, Dr. Robert Strong of Willow Grove moved that the *Complaint* be dismissed.

Dr. Ned B. Stonehouse of Westminster Seminary then delivered a lengthy address designed to show that the evidence which the complainants had presented to the presbytery in the *Complaint* established their claim that various views of Dr. Clark were contrary to Scripture and the subordinate standards of the church and that therefore presbytery should make amends by granting the pleas of the *Complaint*. He also attempted to prove that the proposed *Answer* to the *Complaint*, rather than setting aside the contentions of the *Complaint*, actually went far in confirming its substantial validity.

Dr. Stonehouse accused the proposed *Answer* of failing to set forth accurately the theology of the *Complaint* and asserted that many of the charges of misrepresentations of Dr. Clark's views "would also fall to the ground upon a more careful reading of the *Complaint.*" The *Answer,* moreover, "leaves no doubt that there is a real difference between the theology of the *Complaint* and the theology of Dr. Clark." He denied that the issue revolves about Dr. Clark's declaration that he "accepts the *Westminster Confession of Faith.* To say that is to make subscription to our standards a mere formality." He also denied that the issue was one of apologetics or that the complainants were insisting on subscription to a particular apologetic. "Rather," he said, "we are insisting that theology shall be truly Scriptural, and that there shall be no compromise with rationalism at any point."

Dr. Stonehouse then discussed in considerable detail the doctrine of the knowledge of God. As there are two levels of being, the Creator level and the creature level, so there are two levels of knowledge, and man's knowledge must necessarily always be analogical to God's knowledge. "Truth is one. And man may and does know the same truth that is in the divine mind because of his likeness to God and because of the fact of divine revelation." But God is also incomprehensible, even when truly known, since his revelation of himself is always a revelation to a finite creature and is therefore a condescension to man's finite capacities.

Dr. Stonehouse then discussed the concept of analogy, and stated that, since Dr. Clark "repudiates the doctrine that man's knowledge of a particular proposition necessarily is on a lower level than God's knowledge of the same proposition, and insists that knowledge of propositions must be identical for God and man, it is clear that he holds a view of this doctrine sharply at variance with the Reformed doctrine." He cited quotations from Dr. William Brenton Greene, to whom the *Answer* had made strong appeal in support of its concept of divine incomprehensibility, to prove that Dr. Greene actually held to the view of the complainants.

The proposed *Answer* strongly emphasizes that Dr. Clark holds that "the manner of God's knowing, an eternal intuition, is impossible for man." Dr. Stonehouse acknowledged this and agreed with it, but declared that "a mere distinction as to how knowledge is possessed does not demand the conclusion that the content of knowledge differs." He also held to be inadequate Dr. Clark's contention that God's knowledge differs from man's because God knows all the implications of any proposition, for it is a fact that even the human mind cannot know it as a bare proposition, apart from an actual understanding of implications. "The revelation of it to man brings knowledge of it, but the divine knowledge of it necessarily stands on a different level.... The distinction drawn between propositions and their implications does not as such establish a qualitative difference between the knowledge which God possesses and that which is possible to man."

Dr. Stonehouse attacked as inadequate Dr. Clark's introduction of "infinity" into his formulation of this doctrine. For Dr. Clark, he said, it is only the infinite number of propositions which God knows which stands between man and the possibility of an exhaustive knowledge of the content of the divine mind.

Dr. Stonehouse concluded his address with a detailed consideration of the *Answer*'s treatment of a large number of Scripture passages dealing with the doctrine under scrutiny. He maintained that the interpretation and exegesis of the *Answer* were faulty and inadequate, and attempted to prove that these passages of Scripture, far from supporting Dr. Clark's position, really supported the position of the *Complaint*. In numerous instances he appealed to commentators in support of his contentions.

Dr. Stonehouse was followed immediately by the Rev. Floyd E. Hamilton, who, throughout the debate, appeared to be the best informed protagonist of the theology of Dr. Clark. "There is still misunderstanding," he declared, "in the minds of the complainants regarding Dr. Clark's position." To try to clear up that misunderstanding, he read the following statement, prepared by him and approved by Dr. Clark as being in agreement with his position:

"The position of the complainants regarding the incomprehensibility of God seems to be that incomprehensibility is an incommunicable and unchangable attribute of God that existed before the creation of men or angels, and is not in any way affected by revelation to man or by man's understanding that revelation. No matter how much man may come to know about God throughout eternity, God will be just as incomprehensible and his knowledge will be just as incomprehensible to man after aeons in eternity as it is today. God's knowledge and his incomprehensibility are on a different plane from man's knowledge and are not in any way affected by the knowledge which he may come to enjoy of God's revelation. They therefore hold that it is an error to speak of God's being 'incomprehensible except as he reveals truths concerning his nature.' In using the word 'except,' it is claimed that we are impinging on the majesty of God and bringing him down to the level of the creature.

"It would seem that in using the term *incomprehensible* in this way the complainants are really confusing incomprehensibility with God's omniscience and knowledge, and adding the content of these terms to the meaning of incomprehensibility. It is perfectly true that God's omniscience and knowledge do not change in any way through the process of revelation, and all the knowledge that man may come to enjoy about God throughout eternity would not change God's omniscience in any way. Man could not become omniscient without becoming God. God was omniscient before creation, and his attribute of omniscience is not affected by revelation or by the increase in man's knowledge. But that is an entirely different thing from saying that God is incomprehensible. The moment this word is used it has a double reference, namely, toward man as well as toward God. Its principal reference, however, is toward man and has to do with what man knows about God.

"Now there are two meanings of the word *comprehend*. It means first, *to apprehend*, or *to understand*, and to say that God is incomprehensible in this sense is to say that man cannot understand him. He becomes comprehensible to man, in proportion as man understands the revelations which God gives to man about his nature or knowledge. It is in this sense that the *Answer* declares that God's nature is incomprehensible to man except as God reveals truth to man concerning his own nature.

"The other meaning of the word *comprehend* is *to have complete and exhaustive knowledge* of an object and to place a limit around that which is comprehended, so that everything about it is included in that limit. To say that God's knowledge is incomprehensible in this sense of course is to say that man can never place limits around the knowledge of God and can never have a complete and exhaustive knowledge of any phase of his knowledge, for in order to have such knowledge man would have to know as God knows, with the same mode of knowing, as well as to know the knowledge God has in all its relationships and implications. It would be correct to say that God's knowledge of any truth is always incomprehensible to man in this sense, for if it were comprehensible in that sense, man would have to know it as God knows it, and to know all that God knows about it, that is, to know all its implications and relationships to other truth. It would also be true to say that God's knowledge of a truth is a unitary thing, so that the mode of his knowing, the implications and relationships to other truth all color his knowledge of the meaning of any individual truth. To say that, however, is really to confuse the implications, relationships and mode of knowing with the specific meaning of the truth itself.

"Now Dr. Clark's position is that if man comprehends, or understands the meaning of any truth, truly, the meaning is the same for both God and man. That meaning is not incomprehensible for man in one sense, for man understands the meaning God places on the truth revealed to man. That meaning is the same for God and man. In the other sense, however, God's knowledge of the truth is incomprehensible to man even when the meaning is the same for God and man, for God's knowledge of the truth is God's mode of knowing the truth in all its relationships and implications.

"It seems quite evident that there are two confusions in the minds of the complainants regarding these matters: (1) In the first place they assert of incomprehensibility what is true of omniscience when they say that God was incomprehensible before his works of creation. (2) At the same time they confuse the two meanings of *incomprehensible*, so that when the *Answer* uses the term in one sense they, *i.e.*, the complainants, deny that position while they really have in mind the other meaning of the word *incomprehensible*. For example, God's knowledge of the Trinity is incomprehensible to man, in the sense that man can never understand it in all its implications and relationships and cannot enter into the

86

self-consciousness of God. That knowledge will always be incomprehensible to man in these senses. However, at the same time man can comprehend, *i.e.*, understand, any revelations God may choose to give man about the Trinity, and those revelations have the same meaning for both God and man.

"Now there are two levels of knowledge, one for God and the other for man, but there are not two levels of truth. The *Complaint* teaches that there are two levels of truth when they assert that the meaning of a proposition is different for man and for God and that these meanings do not coincide at any point. Dr. Clark's position is that while God's knowledge is always incomprehensible to man on God's level of knowing, man's knowledge of a truth, if it is correct, is true for both God and man. In other words, man's level of knowledge is always accessible to God, for God is the creator and preserver and controller of man; but God's level of knowledge is inaccessible and therefore incomprehensible to man. God, however, has revealed facts about his knowledge to man, and when they are revealed, and understood by man, they are true for both God and man and have the same meaning for both God and man. God has brought the revelation of his truth down to man's level so that man can know it, without bringing his, *i.e.*, God's, knowledge of the truth down to man's level."

Mr. Hamilton asserted that the *Complaint* talks about "analogical truth," not about "knowing truth analogically." This statement was challenged by the complainants and proven contrary to the facts. Mr. Hamilton then declared that he had isolated fifty-seven separate misrepresentations of Dr. Clark's position in the text of the *Complaint*. Since some of these were called to the complainants' attention by Dr. Clark at the November meeting of presbytery, Mr. Hamilton contended that the complainants should not have printed nor circulated the *Complaint* until after an attempt had been made in conference with Dr. Clark to clear up those points.

Mr. Hamilton then enumerated some of the fifty-seven alleged errors. He insisted that Dr. Clark does not hold that all truth in the divine mind is always propositional; that Dr. Clark does not hold that the divine knowledge consists of an infinite number of propositions, but rather that God can adduce an infinite number of propositions from his knowledge. He said that the *Complaint* was "almost libelous" when it averred that "his [Dr. Clark's] approach…is to a large extent rationalistic." He also charged the *Complaint* with being "insulting" when it declared that, at his July examination in theology, Dr. Clark "studiously avoided answering" a question as to whether there was any faculty in God which is neither intellectual nor volitional and which underlies or accompanies volitional activity. It was later pointed out by the Rev. Arthur W. Kuschke that the complainants did not feel that Dr. Clark was deceptively trying to avoid answering the question, or that he was afraid to answer it, but only that he preferred not to answer it either because he believed it irrelevant or that it would divert attention from what he considered the main matter. No insult was intended or implied.

Dr. William E. Welmers clarified the complainants' position on the matter of analogy and emphatically denied that the *Complaint* taught a doctrine of two levels of truth.

Dr. Stonehouse pointed out that the *Complaint* did not ask for endorsement of the entire contents of the document, but only for action on certain pleas, whereas the *Answer* was framed with a view to becoming in its entirety the *Answer* of the presbytery. The presbytery, he said, has not yet faced the question of what it will do with that *Answer*, nor had Mr. Hamilton really joined issue with the formulation of Dr. Clark's position as given in Dr. Stonehouse's opening address of the debate.

Mr. Hamilton made brief reply to Dr. Stonehouse, after which Mr. Kuschke discussed at considerable length the twin problems of emotions in God and the primacy of the intellect in man. The *Complaint*, he said, denied that God had emotions in the sense of agitations, but again Mr. Kuschke asked the question whether there was any faculty in God, distinct from the intellectual and the volitional, which gives rise to volition. When Scripture says that "God so loved the world…" does the word "loved" mean only something volitional, a matter of mere unemotional choice? Or does God really love men in the sense of having real feelings of compassion and pity for them? "When Dr. Clark says God's love is a volition," declared Mr. Kuschke, "and then speaks of God's faculties as comprising intellect and will, it is to be feared that he falls far short of the meaning of God's love. The complainants are extremely anxious that Dr. Clark should not detract from the love of God. They don't care what name he gives to God's love, but they are concerned that the compassion and tender mercy of God be not denied."

The complainants believe, said Mr. Kuschke, that God does have feelings which are analogous to ours. He quoted 1 *John* 4:7-10. "Each instance of the word 'love' in this quotation, with respect to God's love and man's, is of the same Greek words. Surely at this place in his Word God means to ascribe to himself true feelings and true love which are analogous to feelings and love in us. This we fear Dr. Clark denies."

Dr. Clark defines the apex of religious activity, declared Mr. Kuschke, in terms of intellectual contemplation of

God. In contrast, the complainants hold that glorify-
ing God is the total response of man's whole being to
God's manifestation of his perfections. "Obedience and
love to God," said Mr. Kuschke, "are not less important
than intellectual contemplation; they are not on a lower
plane." Moreover, according to Mr. Kuschke, "Dr. Clark
regards man's intellect as occupying such high rank that
the understanding of the natural man can grasp the
meaning of the words 'Christ died for sinners' 'with the
same ease' as the born-again man. If that is the case, the
understanding does not need to undergo renewal like
the rest of the human personality." Mr. Kuschke quoted
and discussed at length the statement of the proposed
Answer that "regeneration, in spite of the theory of the
Complaint, is not a change in the understanding of these
words [Christ died for sinners]." He pointed out that the
Bible teaches that all of man's faculties are corrupted
by sin, and that every imagination of the thoughts of
man's heart is only evil continually. "If regeneration
did not change our understanding of the words 'Christ
died for sinners,'" he declared, "then we would never be
saved!" He concluded his address in these words: "Thus
Dr. Clark's doctrine of man, both as to the faculties of
the soul and as to the pervasive corruption of original
sin, is wrong, because contrary to the Bible and our
standards. For the fallen human intellect is corrupt and
blind; without the new birth the intellect is unable to
understand the things of God. And the Christian ideal,
even for the hereafter, is not intellectual contemplation,
but rather the total response of man's entire being to
God's revelation of his glory."

Dr. Clark then spoke for the first time and denied that
he held to "identity of man's and God's knowledge."
As for the quotation from Dr. Greene, adduced by Dr.
Stonehouse to show that Dr. Greene did not support the

Answer's view of incomprehensibility, Dr. Clark said that he agreed with the quotation. On the subject of emotions, he said, "If you take the trouble to find out what I mean by *emotions*, God certainly has none."

Dr. Cornelius Van Til of Westminster Seminary then made a plea for a serious consideration of the *Complaint*, despite Mr. Hamilton's alleged fifty-seven varieties of error. He made a masterful exposition of the meaning of analogy and its inherent proof of incomprehensibility. He added further light on the issue of the primacy of the intellect, declaring that it was no mere matter of a difference in terminology.

After Dr. Van Til's speech, Dr. Clark moved the previous question, which, if it had passed, would have forced an immediate vote on the motion to dismiss the *Complaint*. Dr. Clark's motion was lost. He followed with a declaration that Dr. Van Til had tried to equate his position on the matter under discussion with that of Plato. Dr. Clark repudiated vigorously the position Dr. Van Til had outlined, said that he had time and again denied it, and that not one shred of evidence had been adduced to prove that Dr. Van Til was right in his allegations.

Professor Woolley then briefly discussed the question of the legality of the July 7th meeting, and followed this with a discussion of the effect upon the witness of the church that would result from any attempt to carry through the Clarkian emphasis on the primacy of the intellect to its logical conclusion. He cited the history of the development of the New England theology as proof of the devastation that would follow an insistence upon making logical consistency the final test of doctrine, and said that now was the time for this tendency to be nipped in the bud.

Professor R. B. Kuiper discussed Dr. Clark's attempt to solve the paradoxes of divine sovereignty and human responsibility and the decree of reprobation and the universal sincere offer of the Gospel. He said that Dr. Clark does not recognize that there are paradoxes which are intrinsically paradoxical to man because of his very finiteness. A doctrine, said Professor Kuiper, may be revealed in Scripture and yet the human mind be incapable of fully comprehending it. This is a far cry from the notion that God is incomprehensible except as he reveals truths concerning his own nature and that when the Scriptures teach that God is unsearchable, they mean merely that God is unsearchable in so far as man by his own unaided efforts cannot search out his understanding.

Dr. Clark made brief and violent reply in which he designated the attack on his position as "a matter of persistent misrepresentation. The *Answer* is printed," he said, "and I have nothing further to say."

A substitute motion, that the *Answer* of the committee be made the *Answer* of the presbytery, was defeated as a substitute. The previous question was again moved and again failed to carry by the needed two-thirds vote, so that debate was continued.

The Rev. George W. Marston re-read the statement which Mr. Hamilton had prepared and with which Dr. Clark had expressed himself in agreement, and asked the complainants to comment upon it. The Rev. Leslie W. Sloat objected that an *Answer* had been prepared by the committee but that the committee had made no attempt to have its printed *Answer* considered for adoption; instead, a wholly new document which no one had an opportunity to study had been introduced by one individual, and the complainants were now being asked to discuss it as representing Dr. Clark's position.

The Rev. Franklin S. Dyrness said, "We should be sane and sensible in facing this matter." He declared that the presbytery was not in session to consider the *Answer* but to examine the *Complaint*. The presbytery had really been indulging in a re-examination of Dr. Clark. He referred to Mr. Hamilton's allegation of fifty-seven errors in the *Complaint* and to a previous speaker's statement that they were not in reality of central importance. "If those items were not important," he asked, "why did the complainants put them in the *Complaint*?" He cited Dr. Clark's denial that the *Complaint* gives a fair representation of his position, and pled for fairness and honesty.

Mr. Marston felt that, while the *Complaint* and the *Answer* had been widely circulated, the presbyters had never had what they really needed most – an opportunity for each one to have his own copy of the transcript of the record of Dr. Clark's theological examination, on which both the *Complaint* and the *Answer* had been based. "Without it," he asked, "how can we judge?"

After recessing for dinner, the presbytery voted down a motion to postpone further consideration until after mimeographing and circulating the written speeches which had been delivered by several of the complainants and by Mr. Hamilton.

Mr. Hamilton then again arose to deliver another paper on the relation between regeneration and human understanding, which again he said had received Dr. Clark's approval. Confusion was injected, however, by the interpolation of some of Mr. Hamilton's own observations which had not been approved by Dr. Clark. In the course of the speech, Mr. Hamilton declared that *notitia* (knowledge) and *assensus* (assent) could be possessed by the unregenerate man but that *fiducia* (trust) could not. There are three theological terms to designate the three elements of saving faith. Mr. Hamilton was promptly challenged for holding that the unregenerate man possesses two-thirds of the elements of saving faith. On this position, said the complainants, the only thing wrong with the unregenerate man is that his saving faith is one-third incomplete. Moreover, since the *Answer* terms assent the central element in faith, the unregenerate man might then, on Mr. Hamilton's position, be said to possess the central element of saving faith.

Mr. Hamilton then said that he had just been told that Dr. Clark would not agree that the unregenerate man was in possession of the first two of the three elements, but only of the first. It then became clear that this portion of Mr. Hamilton's speech was his own interpolation and had not received Dr. Clark's agreement. It seemed also that Mr. Tichenor, chairman of the committee, held to a different conception of the subject from that which had been defended by Mr. Hamilton.

The supporters of Dr. Clark's theory made valiant efforts to defend the statement of the *Answer* that "regeneration…is not a change in the understanding of these words [Christ died for sinners]." Mr. Kuschke, on the other hand, defended the position of the *Complaint* and pointed out that, when content is injected into the sentence, the unregenerate man must invariably inject the wrong content and the regenerate man the true content.

The complainants' contention that Dr. Clark apparently was reluctant to characterize the free offer of the Gospel as "sincere" was discussed after Dr. Clark had left the meeting. In the course of debate Mr. Tichenor said that in his own opinion Dr. Clark would probably interpret as referring only to the elect the following two passages: "God our Saviour, who will have all men to be saved, and to come unto the knowledge of the truth" (1 *Timothy* 2:3, 4) and "As I live, saith the Lord God, I have no pleasure in the death of the wicked; but that the wicked turn from his way and live: Turn ye, turn ye from your evil ways; for why will ye die, O house of Israel?" (*Ezekiel* 33:11).

Dr. Edward J. Young of Westminster Seminary gave a detailed and carefully worked out exegesis of many of the Old Testament passages dealing with the doctrine of incomprehensibility, but lack of space forbids an inclusion of them in this report.

The question was again called for. Professor Woolley had already reminded the presbyters that they should vote for the motion to dismiss the *Complaint* only if they were completely satisfied that Dr. Clark's theology was a proper presentation of the Reformed Faith.

A roll call vote was taken, showing a tie vote of twenty to twenty, which meant that the motion to dismiss the *Complaint* was lost.

Since there was obviously little chance of completing the business of the presbytery at this session, the meeting was adjourned until 11 a.m. on Thursday, March 29th.

———

After reading the above report, we are still of the opinion that the issues involved in the Clark controversy are matters for discussion by a theological conference rather than grounds of complaint against the licensure and ordination of a candidate for the ministry.

17. The General Assembly's Decisions

Our readers will, no doubt, be interested to know the decision reached by the General Assembly of the Orthodox Presbyterian Church *in re* the *Complaint* against the licensure and ordination of Dr. Gordon H. Clark by the Presbytery of Philadelphia, a case we discussed rather elaborately in our paper more than a year ago.

A year ago, the Twelfth General Assembly appointed a committee to investigate the doctrinal implications of the *Complaint*. This committee had finished its work and presented its report to the Thirteenth General Assembly that convened last May.

A few weeks previous to the convocation of the Assembly a copy of the report prepared on this matter by the committee was sent to me, presumably by some member of the committee. The sender may hereby accept my hearty thanks for the courtesy.

A majority and minority report were offered, the latter by only one member of the committee, Dr. John Murray. It is evident that both the majority and the minority section of the committee took their work very seriously, made a thorough investigation of the matter, and presented their conclusions upon the basis of rather elaborate and, in the main, sound argumentation. The majority report, while expressing doubt with regard to some of Dr. Clark's replies to questions put to him in his examination by the Presbytery of Philadelphia, denied the arguments of the *Complaint* and found no grounds for condemning the action of the Presbytery in licensing Dr. Clark. The report of the minority does not differ radically with that of the majority. It does not take the position that Dr. Clark errs or that the Presbytery of Philadelphia should have found sufficient ground in the examination to refuse his licensure. It rather holds that the examination of Dr. Clark was insufficient to decide upon his licensure and ordination, and that the Presbytery erred in not continuing the examination till sufficient clarity was obtained. Both reports together cover forty long mimeographed sheets, and required three hours to read to the Assembly.

As to the action of the Thirteenth General Assembly in this case, we quote from *The Presbyterian Guardian:*

The assembly defeated a motion to find grounds for complaint against the presbytery's action in approving Dr. Clark's examination in theology and licensing him to preach the Gospel; it passed a motion finding grounds for complaint in the matter of the ordination of Dr. Clark, since in this action presbytery had not observed the provisions of the *Form of Government* which call for a period of time between licensure and ordination.

The latter part of this decision refers to some rule in the *Form of Government* of the Orthodox Presbyterian Church which provides for a certain period of time to elapse between licensure and ordination, and even for a second examination before the ordination, if circumstances require this. The decision reads literally as follows:

> The Assembly finds that there is ground for complaint against the Presbytery of Philadelphia, and declares that the Presbytery of Philadelphia on its meeting of July 7, 1944, erred in the decision to deem the examination for licensure sufficient for ordination and in the decision to ordain Dr. Gordon H. Clark at a subsequent meeting of the Presbytery called for that purpose, in that the Presbytery of Philadelphia failed to observe the plain intent of the provisions of the *Form of Government* XIV, 1; XV, 11, in circumstances which made the propriety of these provisions apparent.

The meaning of these decisions, therefore, is that the *Complaint* is denied, Dr. Clark is maintained in his office as minister, and that the Presbytery of Philadelphia is rebuked for its improper haste to ordain Dr. Clark. The clerk of the General Assembly was instructed to inform the Presbytery of Philadelphia of these decisions, and added to this information the following:

This Assembly also implores the Presbytery of Philadelphia to make acknowledgment of these errors and of
its failure thereby to preserve the peace of the church,
and to report accordingly to the Fourteenth General
Assembly.

The Presbyterian Guardian also informs us that:

When the Assembly defeated the motion to find ground
for complaint in the action of sustaining Dr. Clark's
examination in theology, and proceeded to license him,
a number of commissioners asked that their affirmative
vote be recorded, and these commissioners, together with
others, later filed a formal protest against these decisions
of the Assembly.

While in the main we agree with the decisions of the Assembly on grounds sufficiently set forth in our discussion of
the *Complaint* more than a year ago, we think it regrettable
that the issues involved were not always clearly presented to
and determined by the Thirteenth Assembly. Especially is this
true with regard to the matter of the question concerning the
so-called "general offer of salvation well-meant on the part of
God also to the reprobate." The *Complaint* alleged, and not
without ground, that Dr. Clark denied this well-meaning offer
of salvation to the reprobate.

The committee itself (Majority Report) held rather definite
views on this matter, which, in our opinion, are not Dr. Clark's.
Their conception is expressed in the following paragraph of
their report:

Such passages as *Ezekiel* 18:23 and 33:11 indicate that
God not only delights in the repentance of the actually
penitent but also has that benevolence toward the wicked
whereby he is pleased that they should repent. God not
only delights in the penitent but is also moved by the

riches of his goodness and mercy to desire the repentance and salvation of the impenitent and reprobate. To put this negatively, God does not take delight or pleasure in the death of the wicked. On the contrary, his delight is in mercy. God desires that the reprobate exercise that repentance which they will never exercise and desires for them the enjoyment of good they will never enjoy. And not only so, he desires the exercise of that which they are foreordained not to exercise and he desires for them the enjoyment of good they are foreordained not to enjoy [27].

More boldly the contradiction could not well be stated. Unless in this paragraph the term *foreordination* is to be understood in the Arminian sense, namely, in the sense of reprobation on the ground of foreseen unbelief, this paragraph carries the contradiction into God's very nature: He foreordained what he dislikes; his decree is contrary to his good pleasure. This implies that he must be eternally filled with sorrow over the condition of the wicked in Hell. In our opinion, this is not the teaching of Holy Writ; it is surely not Reformed, but fundamentally Arminian; and we cannot imagine that Dr. Clark would subscribe to this statement. And as to this latter point, the committee itself expresses doubt. We quote from the report:

> It also appears that a question might be raised regarding the answer given by Dr. Clark in reference to the so-called paradox that exists in the offer of salvation to the reprobate: "The solution to that paradox is the distinction between the outward public call and the actual call of the Holy Spirit. The call of the Spirit comes to God's elect only. I don't see a paradox there; it seems perfectly clear to me" [T. 48:2-5].
>
> The Committee cannot regard this solution of the

so-called paradox as an adequate explanation of the problem. The question was: How can God make an offer of salvation to those that are foreordained to damnation? It does not explain the mystery of the co-existence of the full and free offer of salvation and foreordination to damnation to make the obviously necessary distinction between the outward and the inward call. For even after full recognition is given to the truth that God effectually calls only the elect, the mystery of God's will in the offer of salvation to the reprobate still remains [27].

And the Committee concludes its report as follows:

> The Committee has no zeal for the word "paradox." But the Committee believes that great mystery surrounds this matter. Even the reprobate are the objects of divine benevolence, compassion, and lovingkindness, not only in the gifts of this present life such as rain and sunshine, food and raiment, but also in the full and free overtures of God's grace in the gospel. This truth confronts us with the mystery of the divine will, and the believer is overwhelmed with wonder at the unfathomable depths of the divine good pleasure. It may not indeed be said that this mystery should "bother" the believer. It may not even be said that it should cause difficulty for the believer or that the apprehension of this mystery must focus itself in the mind of the believer in the form of an apparent contradiction. But to aver that the distinction between the outward public call and the actual call of the Spirit solves what has been called a "paradox" is, in the judgment of the Committee, to betray a lack of appreciation of the problem involved [28].

We consider it deplorable – not that Dr. Clark was maintained in his office as minister, in spite of the fact that he, according to our conviction, does not agree with the senti-

ments expressed by the Committee – but that these senti-
ments were expressed on the floor of the Assembly, and,
apparently, tacitly assumed to be correct and Reformed or
Calvinistic. For they are most certainly not! It is thus, when
"current opinions" are openly expressed in an official gath-
ering, and tacitly, without further investigation and without
challenge or debate, accepted as the truth, that views, which
are nevertheless errors, come to be looked upon as official
dogmas of the church.

Whether the Orthodox Presbyterian Church wants to adopt
the views expressed by the Committee is not the question now.
But they should not be tacitly accepted.

We deplore that even Dr. Clark, apparently, did not challenge
them. Perhaps, however, the matter may still be clarified at the
next General Assembly, for the Thirteenth Assembly passed
the following resolution:

> Whereas the purity and the peace of the Orthodox
> Presbyterian Church are of the deepest concern to the
> General Assembly, and whereas "to the General Assem-
> bly...belongs the power of deciding in all controversies
> regarding doctrine..." (Form of Government, XI, 5), and
> whereas there has appeared to be a difference in our
> church concerning the Scriptural teaching pertaining
> to the doctrines of the incomprehensibility of God, the
> position of the intellect in relation to other faculties, the
> relation of divine sovereignty and human responsibility,
> and the free offer of the gospel, therefore be it resolved
> that this assembly appoint a committee consisting of
> Messrs. [John] Murray, [Ed] Clowney, R. Gray, W. Young,
> and [Ned] Stonehouse, to study these doctrines in the
> light of Scripture and the Westminster Standards in
> relation to all expressions of views on these doctrines
> that have appeared or may appear in connection with
> the discussion of the Complaint against the Presbytery of

Philadelphia in the matter of the licensure and ordination
of Dr. Gordon H. Clark, in order to clarify these matters,
and report to the Fourteenth General Assembly.

We assure the present Committee of our profound interest
in their labors, and would appreciate deeply to receive from
them a copy of their report when it is ready.

Postscript

IN twenty-five years of publishing the works of Dr. Gordon H. Clark I have encountered a few people – and been told of many more – who dislike Gordon Clark intensely, yet have never read any of his books. In most cases these people have been inoculated against Dr. Clark by Dr. Van Til or his students. It is regrettable that this animosity continues 60 years after the beginning of the Clark-Van Til controversy; it is tragic that the self-professed disciples of Dr. Van Til have continued to slander and misrepresent Dr. Clark and sought to obscure his important contributions to both Christian philosophy and theology. Dr. Hoeksema clearly perceived which party advocated the Biblical position on four major issues in the controversy; it requires extraordinary blindness – or personal loyalty bordering on idolatry – for others not to see so clearly half a century later. We hope that this small book will aid their understanding, and that they will join us in promoting a consistent, Christian faith. It is our hope that the disciples of Dr. Van Til will finally acknowledge his and their errors in this controversy, and end their opposition to Dr. Clark's Christian philosophy.

John Robbins

Scripture Index

Index

    17, 20-23, 82, 84-86, 92, 95, 101
infinity 19
Institutes of the Christian Religion
    (Calvin) 30, 63, 65-66, 69
intellect 9, 14, 25-26, 30, 32, 90,
    101; primacy of 26, 29, 89, 91
intellectual 14, 24-25, 27, 32-33,
    88-89
intelligence 20
intuition 22, 83
irrationalism 50-51, 73
Isaiah 74
Israel 65, 73-74, 78, 95

Jacob 73, 78
Jesus Christ; atonement of 16, 54;
    belief in 48; death of 17; elec-
    tion in 17; faith in 15-16; offer
    of salvation 46; propitiation
    17; salvation by 52; Saviour 77;
    teachings of 76; teaching with
    parables 75
John 17, 77
Judea 63, 71
justification 44

Kellogg, Edward L. 80
kingdom of God 77-78
kingdom of Heaven 75, 77
knowledge 14, 31, 49, 71, 82-83, 85,
    87, 90, 93; divine 21
Kuiper, Herman 67-68, 72
Kuiper, R. B. 13, 91, 92
Kuschke, Arthur W. 88-90, 94
Kuyper, Abraham 32-33, 34, 42,
    67, 69, 70; *Dictaten Dogmatiek,
    Locus de Deo* 32, 42
law 59
liberalism 7

licensure of Gordon Clark 13, 14,
    29, 33, 80, 95, 97, 102
life, eternal 15, 54, 61-62, 70
likeness 82
logic 20, 38-39, 51; *see also* impli-
    cations, rationality, reason
love 26-27, 29-30

Machen, J. Gresham 7, 8, 9
man 90; faculties of 90; finite
    capacities of 82; freedom of 41,
    44; image of God 58; knowl-
    edge of 82, 90; nature of 25,
    26, 31; responsibility of 33-34,
    36, 38-39, 40; sinfulness of 15;
    unregenerate 93-94; *see also*
    image of God, psychology
Marston, George W. 92-93
meaning 18-19, 21-24
memory 46
mercy 27, 64
mind 20, 39, 92; *see also* intellect
miracles 63
modernism 7
moral acts 40
moral law 44
Moses 65
Murray, John 96, 101
mystery 21, 75, 100
mysticism 32-33

National Union of Christian
    Schools 81
nature of God 25, 27-28, 85
New England theology 91
Ninevites 60, 63
nonsense 39
notions 31
notitia 93
nous 31

The Crisis of Our Time

HISTORIANS have christened the thirteenth century the Age of Faith and termed the eighteenth century the Age of Reason. The present age has been called many things: the Atomic Age, the Age of Inflation, the Age of the Tyrant, the Age of Aquarius; but it deserves one name more than the others: the Age of Irrationalism. Contemporary secular intellectuals are anti-intellectual. Contemporary philosophers are anti-philosophy. Contemporary theologians are anti-theology.

In past centuries, secular philosophers have generally believed that knowledge is possible to man. Consequently they expended a great deal of thought and effort trying to justify knowledge. In the twentieth century, however, the optimism of the secular philosophers all but disappeared. They despaired of knowledge.

Like their secular counterparts, the great theologians and doctors of the church taught that knowledge is possible to man. Yet the theologians of the present age also repudiated that belief. They too despaired of knowledge. This radical skepticism has penetrated our entire culture, from television to music to literature. *The Christian at the beginning of the twenty-first century is confronted with an overwhelming cultural consensus – sometimes stated explicitly but most often implicitly: Man does not and cannot know anything truly.*

What does this have to do with Christianity? Simply this: If man can know nothing truly, man can truly know nothing. We cannot know that the Bible is the Word of God, that Christ died for his people, or that Christ is alive today at the right hand of the Father. Unless knowledge is possible, Christianity is nonsensical, for it claims to be knowledge. What is at stake at the beginning of the twenty-first century is not simply a single doctrine, such as the virgin birth, or the existence of Hell, as important as those doctrines may be, but the whole of Christianity itself. If knowledge is not possible to man, it is worse than silly to argue points of doctrine – it is insane.

The irrationalism of the present age is so thoroughgoing and pervasive that even the Remnant – the segment of the professing church that remains faithful – has accepted much of it, frequently without even being aware of what it is accepting. In some religious circles this irrationalism has become synonymous with piety and humility, and those who oppose it are denounced as rationalists, as though to be logical were a sin. Our contemporary anti-theologians make a contradiction and call it a Mystery. The faithful ask for truth and are given Paradox and Antinomy. If any balk at swallowing the absurdities of the anti-theologians who teach in the seminaries or have graduated from the seminaries, they are frequently marked as heretics or schismatics who seek to act independently of God.

There is no greater threat facing the church of Christ at this moment than the irrationalism that now controls our entire culture. Totalitarianism, guilty of tens of millions of murders – including those of millions of Christians – is to be feared, but not nearly so much as the idea that we do not and cannot know the literal truth. Hedonism, the popular philosophy of America, is not to be feared so much as the belief that logic

– that "mere human logic," to use the religious irrationalists' own phrase – is futile. The attacks on truth, on knowledge, on propositional revelation, on the intellect, on words, and on logic are renewed daily. But note well: The misologists – the haters of logic – use logic to demonstrate the futility of using logic. The anti-intellectuals construct intricate intellectual arguments to prove the insufficiency of the intellect. Those who deny the competence of words to express thought use words to express their thoughts. The proponents of poetry, myth, metaphor, and analogy argue for their theories by using literal prose, whose competence – even whose possibility – they deny. The anti-theologians use the revealed Word of God to show that there can be no revealed Word of God – or that if there could, it would remain impenetrable darkness and Mystery to our finite minds.

Nonsense Has Come

Is it any wonder that the world is grasping at straws – the straws of experientialism, mysticism, and drugs? After all, if people are told that the Bible contains insoluble mysteries, then is not a flight into mysticism to be expected? On what grounds can it be condemned? Certainly not on logical grounds or Biblical grounds, if logic is futile and the Bible unknowable. Moreover, if it cannot be condemned on logical or Biblical grounds, it cannot be condemned at all. If people are going to have a religion of the mysterious, they will not adopt Christianity: They will have a genuine mystery religion. The popularity of mysticism, drugs, and religious experience is the logical consequence of the irrationalism of the present age. There can and will be no Christian reformation – and no restoration of a free society – unless and until the irrationalism of the age is totally repudiated by Christians.

The Church Defenseless

Yet how shall they do it? The official spokesmen for Christianity have been fatally infected with irrationalism. The seminaries, which annually train thousands of men to teach millions of Christians, are the finishing schools of irrationalism, completing the job begun by the government schools and colleges. Most of the pulpits of the conservative churches (we are not speaking of the obviously apostate churches) are occupied by graduates of the anti-theological schools. These products of modern anti-theological education, when asked to give a reason for the hope that is in them, can generally respond with only the intellectual analogue of a shrug – a mumble about Mystery. They have not grasped – and therefore cannot teach those for whom they are responsible – the first truth: "And you shall know the truth." Many, in fact, explicitly contradict Christ, saying that, at best, we possess only "pointers" to the truth, or something "similar" to the truth, a mere analogy. Is the impotence of the Christian church a puzzle? Is the fascination with Pentecostalism, faith healing, Eastern Orthodoxy, and Roman Catholicism – all sensate and anti-intellectual religions – among members of Christian churches an enigma? Not when one understands the pious nonsense that is purveyed in the name of God in the religious colleges and seminaries.

The Trinity Foundation

The creators of The Trinity Foundation firmly believe that theology is too important to be left to the licensed theologians – the graduates of the schools of theology. They have created The Trinity Foundation for the express purpose of teaching believers all that the Scriptures contain – not warmed over, baptized, Antichristian philosophies. Each member of the board of directors of The Trinity Foundation has signed this oath: "I believe that the Bible alone and the Bible in its entirety is the Word of God and, therefore, inerrant in the autographs. I believe that the system of truth presented in the Bible is best summarized in the *Westminster Confession of Faith*. So help me God."

The ministry of The Trinity Foundation is the presentation of the system of truth taught in Scripture as clearly and as completely as possible. We do not regard obscurity as a virtue, nor confusion as a sign of spirituality. Confusion, like all error, is sin, and teaching that confusion is all that Christians can hope for is doubly sin.

The presentation of the truth of Scripture necessarily involves the rejection of error. The Foundation has exposed and will continue to expose the irrationalism of the present age, whether its current spokesman be an existentialist philosopher or a professed Reformed theologian. We oppose anti-intellectualism, whether it be espoused by a Neo-orthodox theologian or a fundamentalist evangelist. We reject misology, whether it be on the lips of a Neo-evangelical or those of a Roman Catholic Charismatic. We repudiate agnosticism, whether it be secular or religious. To each error we bring the brilliant light of Scripture, proving all things, and holding fast to that which is true.

The Primacy of Theory

The ministry of The Trinity Foundation is not a "practical" ministry. If you are a pastor, we will not enlighten you on how to organize an ecumenical prayer meeting in your community or how to double church attendance in a year. If you are a homemaker, you will have to read elsewhere to find out how to become a total woman. If you are a businessman, we will not tell you how to develop a social conscience. The professing church is drowning in such "practical" advice.

The Trinity Foundation is unapologetically theoretical in its outlook, believing that theory without practice is dead, and that practice without theory is blind. The trouble with the professing church is not primarily in its practice, but in its theory. Churchgoers and teachers do not know, and many do not even care to know, the doctrines of Scripture. Doctrine is intellectual, and churchgoers and teachers are generally anti-intellectual. Doctrine is ivory tower philosophy, and they scorn ivory towers. The ivory tower, however, is the control tower of a civilization. It is a fundamental, theoretical mistake of the "practical" men to think that they can be merely practical, for practice is always the practice of some theory. The relationship between theory and practice is the relationship between cause and effect. If a person believes correct theory, his practice will tend to be correct. The practice of contemporary Christians is immoral because it is the practice of false theories. It is a major theoretical mistake of the "practical" men to think that they can ignore the ivory towers of the philosophers and theologians as irrelevant to their lives. Every action that "practical" men take is governed by the thinking that has occurred in some ivory tower – whether that tower be the British Museum; the Academy; a home in Basel, Switzerland; or a tent in Israel.

In Understanding Be Men

It is the first duty of the Christian to understand correct theory – correct doctrine – and thereby implement correct practice. This order – first theory, then practice – is both logical and Biblical. It is, for example, exhibited in Paul's *Epistle to the Romans,* in which he spends the first eleven chapters expounding theory and the last five discussing practice. The contemporary teachers of Christians have not only reversed the Biblical order, they have inverted the Pauline emphasis on theory and practice. The virtually complete failure of the teachers of the professing church to instruct believers in correct doctrine is the cause of the misconduct and spiritual and cultural impotence of Christians. The church's lack of power is the result of its lack of truth. The *Gospel* is the power of God, not religious experiences or personal relationships. The church has no power because it has abandoned the Gospel, the good news, for a religion of experientialism. Twentieth-first-century American churchgoers are children carried about by every wind of doctrine, not knowing what they believe, or even if they believe anything for certain.

The chief purpose of The Trinity Foundation is to counteract the irrationalism of the age and to expose the errors of the teachers of the church. Our emphasis – on the Bible as the sole source of knowledge, on the primacy of truth, on the supreme importance of correct doctrine, and on the necessity for systematic and logical thinking – is almost unique in Christendom. To the extent that the church survives – and she will survive and flourish – it will be because of her increasing acceptance of these basic ideas and their logical implications.

We believe that The Trinity Foundation is filling a vacuum in Christendom. We are saying that Christianity is intellectually defensible – that, in fact, it is the only intellectually defensible system of thought. We are saying that God has made the wisdom of this world – whether that wisdom be called science, religion, philosophy, or common sense – foolishness. We are appealing to all Christians who have not conceded defeat in the intellectual battle with the world to join us in our efforts to raise a standard to which all men of sound mind can repair.

The love of truth, of God's Word, has all but disappeared

in our time. We are committed to and pray for a great instauration. But though we may not see this reformation in our lifetimes, we believe it is our duty to present the whole counsel of God, because Christ has commanded it. The results of our teaching are in God's hands, not ours. Whatever those results, his Word is never taught in vain, but always accomplishes the result that he intended it to accomplish. Professor Gordon H. Clark has stated our view well:

> There have been times in the history of God's people, for example, in the days of Jeremiah, when refreshing grace and widespread revival were not to be expected: The time was one of chastisement. If this twentieth century is of a similar nature, individual Christians here and there can find comfort and strength in a study of God's Word. But if God has decreed happier days for us, and if we may expect a world-shaking and genuine spiritual awakening, then it is the author's belief that a zeal for souls, however necessary, is not the sufficient condition. Have there not been devout saints in every age, numerous enough to carry on a revival? Twelve such persons are plenty. What distinguishes the arid ages from the period of the Reformation, when nations were moved as they had not been since Paul preached in Ephesus, Corinth, and Rome, is the latter's fullness of knowledge of God's Word. To echo an early Reformation thought, when the ploughman and the garage attendant know the Bible as well as the theologian does, and know it better than some contemporary theologians, then the desired awakening shall have already occurred.

In addition to publishing books, the Foundation publishes a monthly newsletter, *The Trinity Review*. Subscriptions to *The Review* are free to U.S. addresses; please write to the address on the order form to become a subscriber. If you would like further information or would like to support our work, please let us know.

The Trinity Foundation is a non-profit foundation, tax exempt under section 501 (c)(3) of the Internal Revenue Code of 1954. You can help us disseminate the Word of God through your tax-deductible contributions to the Foundation.

JOHN W. ROBBINS

Intellectual Ammunition

T HE Trinity Foundation is committed to bringing every philosophical and theological thought captive to Christ. The books listed below are designed to accomplish that goal. They are written with two subordinate purposes: (1) to demolish all non-Christian claims to knowledge; and (2) to build a system of truth based upon the Bible alone.

Philosophy

Ancient Philosophy
Gordon H. Clark   Trade paperback $24.95
    This book covers the thousand years from the Pre-Socratics to Plotinus. It represents some of the early work of Dr. Clark – the work that made his academic reputation. It is an excellent college text.

Behaviorism and Christianity
Gordon H. Clark   Trade paperback $5.95
    Behaviorism is a critique of both secular and religious behaviorists. It includes chapters on John Watson, Edgar S. Singer, Jr., Gilbert Ryle, B. F. Skinner, and Donald MacKay. Clark's refutation of behaviorism and his argument for a Christian doctrine of man are unanswerable.

Christ and Civilization
John W. Robbins   Trade paperback $3.95

Civilization as we know it is a result of the widespread proclamation and belief of the Gospel of justification by faith alone in the sixteenth century. Christ foretold this result in the Sermon on the Mount: "Seek first the Kingdom of God and his righteousness, and all these things will be added to you."

This brief overview of the history of western civilization makes it clear that our cultural debt is to the Gospel, not to Greece and Rome.

Christian Philosophy   Hardback $29.95
Gordon H. Clark   Trade paperback $21.95

This book, Volume 4 in *The Works of Gordon Haddon Clark*, combines three of his most important works in philosophy: *Three Types of Religious Philosophy*; *Religion, Reason and Revelation*; and *An Introduction to Christian Philosophy*. Together they constitute Dr. Clark's principal statement of his Christian philosophy.

A Christian Philosophy of Education   Hardback $18.95
Gordon H. Clark   Trade paperback $12.95

The first edition of this book was published in 1946. It sparked the contemporary interest in Christian schools. In the 1970s, Dr. Clark thoroughly revised and updated it, and it is needed now more than ever. Its chapters include: The Need for a World-View; The Christian World-View; The Alternative to Christian Theism; Neutrality; Ethics; The Christian Philosophy of Education; Academic Matters; and Kindergarten to University. Three appendices are included: The Relationship of Public Education to Christianity; A Protestant World-View; and Art and the Gospel.

A Christian View of Men and Things   Hardback $29.95
Gordon H. Clark   Trade paperback $18.95
No other book achieves what *A Christian View* does: the presentation of Christianity as it applies to history, politics, ethics, science, religion, and epistemology. Dr. Clark's command of both worldly philosophy and Scripture is evident on every page, and the result is a breathtaking and invigorating challenge to the wisdom of this world. This is Volume 1 in *The Works of Gordon Haddon Clark*.

Clark Speaks from the Grave
Gordon H. Clark   Trade paperback $3.95
Dr. Clark chides some of his critics for their failure to defend Christianity competently. *Clark Speaks* is a stimulating and illuminating discussion of the errors of contemporary apologists.

Ecclesiastical Megalomania: The Economic and Political Thought of the Roman Catholic Church
John W. Robbins   Hardback $29.95
This detailed and thorough analysis and critique of the social teaching of the Roman Church-State is the only such book available by a Christian economist and political philosopher. The book's conclusions reveal the Roman Church-State to be an advocate of its own brand of faith-based fascism. *Ecclesiastical Megalomania* includes the complete text of the *Donation of Constantine* and Lorenzo Valla's exposé of the hoax.

Education, Christianity, and the State
J. Gresham Machen   Trade paperback $10.95
    Machen was one of the foremost educators, theologians,
    and defenders of Christianity in the twentieth century.
    The author of several scholarly books, Machen saw clearly
    that if Christianity is to survive and flourish, a system of
    Christian schools must be established. This collection of
    essays and speeches captures his thoughts on education
    over nearly three decades.

Essays on Ethics and Politics
Gordon H. Clark   Trade paperback $10.95
    Dr. Clark's essays, written over the course of five de-
    cades, are a major statement of Christian ethics.

Gordon H. Clark: Personal Recollections
John W. Robbins, editor   Trade paperback $6.95
    Friends of Dr. Clark have written their recollections
    of the man. Contributors include family members, col-
    leagues, students, and friends such as Harold Lindsell,
    Carl Henry, Ronald Nash, and Anna Marie Hager.

Historiography: Secular and Religious
Gordon H. Clark   Trade paperback $13.95
    In this masterful work, Dr. Clark applies his philoso-
    phy to the writing of history, examining all the major
    schools of historiography.

An Introduction to Christian Philosophy
Gordon H. Clark
    See *Christian Philosophy*.

Language and Theology
Gordon H. Clark   Trade paperback $9.95
   There were two main currents in twentieth-century
philosophy – Language Philosophy and Existentialism.
Both were hostile to Christianity. Dr. Clark disposes of
Language Philosophy in this brilliant critique of Bertrand
Russell, Ludwig Wittgenstein, Rudolf Carnap, A. J. Ayer,
Langdon Gilkey, and many others.

Logic
Gordon H. Clark   Hardback $16.95
   Written as a textbook for Christian schools, *Logic* is
another unique book from Dr. Clark's pen. His presentation of the laws of thought, which must be followed
if Scripture is to be understood correctly, and which are
found in Scripture itself, is both clear and thorough. *Logic*
is an indispensable book for the thinking Christian.

Lord God of Truth, Concerning the Teacher
Gordon H. Clark and
Aurelius Augustine   Trade paperback $7.95
   This essay by Dr. Clark summarizes many of the most
telling arguments against empiricism and defends the
Biblical teaching that we know God and truth imme-
diately. The dialogue by Augustine is a refutation of
empirical language philosophy.

The Philosophy of Science and Belief in God
Gordon H. Clark   Trade paperback $8.95
   In opposing the contemporary idolatry of science, Dr.
Clark analyzes three major aspects of science: the problem
of motion, Newtonian science, and modern theories of
physics. His conclusion is that science, while it may be

useful, is always false; and he demonstrates its falsity in numerous ways. Since science is always false, it can offer no alternative to the Bible and Christianity.

Religion, Reason and Revelation
Gordon H. Clark   Trade paperback $10.95
   One of Dr. Clark's apologetical masterpieces, *Religion, Reason and Revelation* has been praised for the clarity of its thought and language. It includes these chapters: Is Christianity a Religion? Faith and Reason; Inspiration and Language; Revelation and Morality; and God and Evil. It is must reading for all serious Christians.
   See also *Christian Philosophy.*

The Scripturalism of Gordon H. Clark
W. Gary Crampton   Trade paperback $9.95
   Dr. Crampton has written an introduction to the philosophy of Gordon H. Clark that is helpful to both beginners and advanced students of theology. This book includes a bibliography of Dr. Clark's works.

Thales to Dewey:
A History of Philosophy   Hardback $29.95
Gordon H. Clark   Trade paperback $21.95
   This is the best one-volume history of philosophy in print. This is Volume 3 in *The Works of Gordon Haddon Clark.*

Three Types of Religious Philosophy
Gordon H. Clark
   See *Christian Philosophy.*

William James and John Dewey
Gordon H. Clark   Trade paperback $8.95
    William James and John Dewey are two of the most
influential philosophers America has produced. Their
philosophies of instrumentalism and pragmatism are
hostile to Christianity, and Dr. Clark demolishes their
arguments.

Without A Prayer: Ayn Rand and the Close of Her System
John W. Robbins   Hardback $27.95
    Ayn Rand has been a best-selling author since 1957.
Without A Prayer discusses Objectivism's epistemology,
theology, ethics, and politics in detail. Appendices include
analyses of books by Leonard Peikoff and David Kelley, as
well as several essays on Christianity and philosophy.

Theology

Against the Churches: The Trinity Review 1989-1998
John W. Robbins, editor   Oversize hardback $39.95
    This is the second volume of essays from *The Trinity
Review*, covering its second ten years, 1989-1998. This
volume, like the first, is fully indexed and is very useful in
research and in the classroom. Authors include: Gordon
Clark, John Robbins, Charles Hodge, J. C. Ryle, Horatius
Bonar, and Robert L. Dabney.

Against the World: The Trinity Review 1978-1988
John W. Robbins, editor   Oversize hardback $34.95
    This is a clothbound collection of the essays published
in *The Trinity Review* from 1978 to 1988, 70 in all. It is a
valuable source of information and arguments explaining
and defending Christianity.

The Atonement

Gordon H. Clark   Trade paperback $8.95

In *The Atonement,* Dr. Clark discusses the covenants, the virgin birth and incarnation, federal headship and representation, the relationship between God's sovereignty and justice, and much more. He analyzes traditional views of the atonement and criticizes them in the light of Scripture alone.

The Biblical Doctrine of Man

Gordon H. Clark   Trade paperback $6.95

Is man soul and body or soul, spirit, and body? What is the image of God? Is Adam's sin imputed to his children? Is evolution true? Are men totally depraved? What is the heart? These are some of the questions discussed and answered from Scripture in this book.

By Scripture Alone

W. Gary Crampton   Trade paperback $12.95

This is a clear and thorough explanation of the Scriptural doctrine of Scripture and a refutation of the recent Romanist attack on Scripture as the Word of God.

Can the Orthodox Presbyterian Church Be Saved?

John W. Robbins   Trade paperback $3.95

This small book, which demonstrates the central errors of OPC history and theology since the 1940s, is an alarm to awaken members of the OPC from their slumbers.

The Changing of the Guard

Mark W. Karlberg   Trade paperback $3.95

This essay is a critical discussion of Westminster Seminary's anti-Reformational and un-Biblical teaching on the doctrine of justification. Dr. Karlberg exposes the doctrine of justification by faith and works – not *sola fide* – taught at Westminster Seminary for the past 25 years, by Professors Norman Shepherd, Richard Gaffin, John Frame, and others.

Christianity and Neo-Liberalism: The Spiritual Crisis in the Orthodox Presbyterian Church and Beyond
Paul M. Elliott   Trade paperback $19.95
   This massively-documented book details the influence Westminster Theological Seminary has had on the Orthodox Presbyterian Church and other churches and organizations. It is both a work of theological analysis and a call to action.

The Church Effeminate
John W. Robbins, editor   Hardback $29.95
   This is a collection of 39 essays by the best theologians of the church on the doctrine of the church: Martin Luther, John Calvin, Benjamin Warfield, Gordon Clark, J. C. Ryle, and many more. The essays cover the structure, function, and purpose of the church.

The Clark-Van Til Controversy
Herman Hoeksema   Trade paperback $9.95
   This collection of essays by the founder of the Protestant Reformed Churches – essays written at the time of the Clark-Van Til controversy in the 1940s – is one of the best commentaries on those events in print.

A Companion to The Current Justification Controversy
John W. Robbins   Trade paperback $9.95
   This book includes documentary source material not
available in *The Current Justification Controversy*, an
essay tracing the origins and continuation of this controversy throughout American Presbyterian churches,
and an essay on the New Perspective on Paul by Robert
L. Reymond.

Cornelius Van Til: The Man and The Myth
John W. Robbins   Trade paperback $2.45
   The actual teachings of this eminent Philadelphia theo-
logian have been obscured by the myths that surround
him. This book penetrates those myths and criticizes
Van Til's surprisingly unorthodox views of God and the
Bible.

The Current Justification Controversy
O. Palmer Robertson   Trade paperback $9.95
   From 1975 to 1982 a controversy over justification raged
within Westminster Theological Seminary and the Philadelphia Presbytery of the Orthodox Presbyterian Church.
As a member of the faculties of both Westminster and
Covenant Seminaries during this period, O. Palmer Robertson was an important participant in this controversy.
This is his account of the controversy, vital background
for understanding the defection from the Gospel that is
now widespread in Presbyterian churches.

The Everlasting Righteousness
Horatius Bonar   Trade paperback $8.95
   Originally published in 1874, the language of Bonar's
masterpiece on justification by faith alone has been

updated and Americanized for easy reading and clear understanding. This is one of the best books ever written on justification.

See also *Not What My Hands Have Done.*

Faith and Saving Faith
Gordon H. Clark
See *What Is Saving Faith?*

God and Evil: The Problem Solved
Gordon H. Clark   Trade paperback $5.95
This volume is Chapter 5 of *Religion, Reason and Revelation,* in which Dr. Clark presents his solution to the problem of evil.

God-Breathed: The Divine Inspiration of the Bible
Louis Gaussen   Trade paperback $16.95
Gaussen, a nineteenth-century Swiss Reformed pastor, comments on hundreds of passages in which the Bible claims to be the Word of God. This is a massive defense of the doctrine of the plenary and verbal inspiration of Scripture.

God's Hammer: The Bible and Its Critics
Gordon H. Clark   Trade paperback $10.95
The starting point of Christianity, the doctrine on which all other doctrines depend, is "The Bible alone, and the Bible in its entirety, is the Word of God written, and, therefore, inerrant in the autographs." Over the centuries the opponents of Christianity, with Satanic shrewdness, have concentrated their attacks on the truthfulness and completeness of the Bible. In the twentieth century the attack was not so much in the fields of history and ar-

chaeology as in philosophy. Dr. Clark's brilliant defense of the complete truthfulness of the Bible is captured in this collection of eleven major essays.

The Holy Spirit
Gordon H. Clark   Trade paperback $8.95
     This discussion of the third person of the Trinity is both concise and exact. Dr. Clark includes chapters on the work of the Spirit, sanctification, and Pentecostalism.

The Incarnation
Gordon H. Clark   Trade paperback $8.95
     Who is Christ? The attack on the doctrine of the Incarnation in the nineteenth and twentieth centuries was vigorous, but the orthodox response was lame. Dr. Clark reconstructs the doctrine of the Incarnation, building and improving upon the Chalcedonian definition.

The Johannine Logos
Gordon H. Clark   Trade paperback $5.95
     Dr. Clark analyzes the relationship between Christ, who is the truth, and the Bible. He explains why John used the same word to refer to both Christ and his teaching. Chapters deal with the Prologue to John's Gospel; *Logos* and *Rheemata*; Truth; and Saving Faith. See also *What Is Saving Faith?*

Justification by Faith Alone
Charles Hodge   Trade paperback $10.95
     Charles Hodge of Princeton Seminary was the best American theologian of the nineteenth century. Here, for the first time, are his two major essays on justifica-

tion in one volume. This book is essential in defending the faith.

See also *Not What My Hands Have Done.*

Karl Barth's Theological Method
Gordon H. Clark   Trade paperback $18.95
   Karl Barth's Theological Method is perhaps the best critique of the Neo-orthodox theologian Karl Barth ever written. Dr. Clark discusses Barth's view of revelation, language, and Scripture, focusing on his method of writing theology, rather than presenting a comprehensive analysis of the details of Barth's theology.

Logical Criticisms of Textual Criticism
Gordon H. Clark   Trade paperback $3.25
   Dr. Clark's acute mind enables him to demonstrate the inconsistencies, assumptions, and flights of fancy that characterize the science of New Testament criticism.

See also *Commentaries on Paul's Epistles.*

Not Reformed at All:
Medievalsim in "Reformed" Churches
John Robbins and Sean Gerety   Trade paperback $9.95
   This book is a response to and refutation of Douglas Wilson's book *"Reformed" is Not Enough: Recovering the Objectivity of the Covenant.* Wilson, one of the leading figures in the Neolegalist movement in Reformed and Presbyterian circles, attacked covenant theology and proposed a "visible, photographable" covenant which one enters by ritual baptism, making one a Christian. That salvation can be lost by one's own lack of performance or by action of authorized representatives of the church.

This refutation of Wilson is a defense of the Covenant of Grace.

Not What My Hands Have Done
Charles Hodge, Horatius Bonar   Trade paperback $16.95
   This is the combined edition of *Justification by Faith Alone* (by Hodge) and *The Everlasting Righteousness* (by Bonar). Combined, these books offer both an introduction to and an in-depth discussion of the central doctrine of Christianity, justification by faith alone.

Predestination
Gordon H. Clark   Trade paperback $10.95
   Dr. Clark thoroughly discusses one of the most controversial and pervasive doctrines of the Bible: that God is, quite literally, Almighty. Free will, the origin of evil, God's omniscience, creation, and the new birth are all presented within a Scriptural framework. The objections of those who do not believe in Almighty God are considered and refuted. This edition also contains the text of the booklet, *Predestination in the Old Testament*.

Sanctification
Gordon H. Clark   Trade paperback $8.95
   In this book Dr. Clark discusses historical theories of sanctification, the sacraments, and the Biblical doctrine of sanctification.

Study Guide to the Westminster Confession
W. Gary Crampton   Oversize paperback $10.95
   This *Study Guide* can be used by individuals or classes. It contains a paragraph-by-paragraph summary of the

Westminster Confession, and questions for the student to answer. Space for answers is provided. The *Guide* will be most beneficial when used in conjunction with Dr. Clark's *What Do Presbyterians Believe?*

A Theology of the Holy Spirit
Frederick Dale Bruner   Trade paperback $16.95
    First published in 1970, this book has been hailed by reviewers as "thorough," "fair," "comprehensive," "devastating," "the most significant book on the Holy Spirit," and "scholarly." Gordon Clark described this book in his own book *The Holy Spirit* as "a masterly and exceedingly well researched exposition of Pentecostalism. The documentation is superb, as is also his penetrating analysis of their non-scriptural and sometimes contradictory conclusions." Unfortunately, the book is marred by the author's sacramentarianism.

The Trinity
Gordon H. Clark   Trade paperback $8.95
    Apart from the doctrine of Scripture, no teaching of the Bible is more fundamental than the doctrine of God. Dr. Clark's defense of the orthodox doctrine of the Trinity is a principal portion of his systematic theology. There are chapters on the Deity of Christ; Augustine; the Incomprehensibility of God; Bavinck and Van Til; and the Holy Spirit; among others.

What Calvin Says
W. Gary Crampton   Trade paperback $10.95
    This is a clear, readable, and thorough introduction to the theology of John Calvin.

What Do Presbyterians Believe?
Gordon H. Clark   Trade paperback $10.95
   This classic is the best commentary on the *Westminster Confession of Faith* ever written.

What Is Saving Faith?
Gordon H. Clark   Trade paperback $12.95
   This is the combined edition of *Faith and Saving Faith* and *The Johannine Logos.* The views of the Roman Catholic Church, John Calvin, Thomas Manton, John Owen, Charles Hodge, and B. B. Warfield are discussed in this book. Is the object of faith a person or a proposition? Is faith more than belief? Is belief thinking with assent, as Augustine said? In a world chaotic with differing views of faith, Dr. Clark clearly explains the Biblical view of faith and saving faith.
   In *The Johannine Logos*, Dr. Clark analyzes the relationship between Christ, who is the truth, and the Bible. He explains why John used the same word to refer to both Christ and his teaching. Chapters deal with the Prologue to John's Gospel; *Logos* and *Rheemata;* Truth; and Saving Faith.

Clark's Commentaries
on the New Testament

Colossians	Trade paperback	$6.95
Commentaries on Paul's Letters		
(Colossians, Ephesians, 1 and 2		
Thessalonians, Logical Criticisms	Hardback	$29.95
of Textual Criticism)	Trade paperback	$21.95
First Corinthians	Trade paperback	$10.95
First John	Trade paperback	$10.95

New Heavens, New Earth
   (*First* and *Second Peter*)   Trade paperback $10.95
The Pastoral Epistles   Hardback $29.95
   (*1* and *2 Timothy* and *Titus*)   Trade paperback $14.95
Philippians   Trade paperback $9.95

All of Clark's commentaries are expository, not technical, and are written for the Christian layman. His purpose is to explain the text clearly and accurately so that the Word of God will be thoroughly known by every Christian.

The Trinity Library

We will send you one copy of each of the books listed above for $500 (retail value $800), postpaid to any address in the U.S. You may also order the books you want individually on the order form on the next page. Because some of the books are in short supply, we must reserve the right to substitute others of equal or greater value in The Trinity Library. This special offer expires October 31, 2008.

Order Form

NAME   _____

ADDRESS   _____

                 _____

TELEPHONE   _____

E-MAIL _____

Please:

❑ add my name to the mailing list for *The Trinity Review*. I understand that there is no charge for single copies of *The Review* sent to a U. S. address.

❑ accept my tax deductible contribution of $_____ .

❑ send me _____ copies of *The Clark-Van Til Controversy*. I enclose as payment U. S. $_____.

❑ send me the Trinity Library. I enclose U. S. $500 as full payment.

❑ send me the following books. I enclose full payment in the amount of $_____ for them.

_____

_____

_____

_____

The Trinity Foundation
Post Office Box 68
Unicoi, Tennessee 37692
Website: http://www.trinityfoundation.org/
United States of America

Shipping: Please add $6.00 for the first book, and 50 cents for each additional book. For foreign orders, please add $1.00 for each additional book.